EX LIBRIS

A SUSSEX GUIDE

SUSSEX WOMEN

ANN KRAMER

Illustrated by
IVAN HISSEY

SNAKE RIVER PRESS

SNAKE RIVER PRESS

Book No 8
Books about Sussex for the enthusiast

Published in 2007 by
SNAKE RIVER PRESS
South Downs Way, Alfriston, Sussex BN26 5XW
www.snakeriverpress.co.uk

ISBN 978-1-906022-07-5

This book was conceived, designed and produced by
SNAKE RIVER PRESS

ART DIRECTOR & PUBLISHER *Peter Bridgewater*
EDITORIAL DIRECTOR *Viv Croot*
EDITOR *Mandy Greenfield*
PAGE MAKEUP *Richard Constable & Chris Morris*
ILLUSTRATOR *Ivan Hissey*
CONSULTANT *Lorraine Harrison*

This book is typeset in Perpetua & Gill Sans,
two fonts designed by Eric Gill

Printed and bound in China

DEDICATION

To Sarah Kramer, my Sussex-born daughter

CONTENTS

INTRODUCTION

'Whatever women do they must do twice as well as men to be thought half as good. Luckily, this is not difficult'.
CHARLOTTE WHITTON, 1896-1975, *CANADA MONTH, JUNE 1963*

This book presents the stories of 30 Sussex women. They are quite an eclectic group: included here are writers, artists and musicians; reformers, campaigners and philanthropists; entertainers, aristocrats and commoners. What unites them is that they are all women and that they were either born in Sussex or were drawn to the county for one reason or another. Another unifying feature is that all of them made a considerable impact on their community or society at large, which in some cases continues to this day.

Interestingly, and at the risk of over-generalising, modern guidebooks on Sussex do not include many women. This is strange, but not necessarily unusual. Even in the 21st century women still do not always get the same coverage as men, and some of the women included here are not household names, although they should be. But there are well-known women in this book: the artist Vanessa Bell, for example, is included, and her links to Sussex via her country retreat at Charleston are well established. Likewise her sister, the writer Virginia Woolf, whose connections to Sussex (not least her tragic death in the county) are well known, has a place in this book. Although neither woman was Sussex-born, they both spent a lot of time in the county, which offered them inspiration, a peaceful retreat from London and a place where they could write, paint or socialise. Virginia Woolf wrote some of her most original work in her back garden at Monk's House at Rodmell.

Other women in this book certainly deserve to be better known. Many were during their lifetimes, but have subsequently fallen out of fashion or been shunted into the backwaters of history. Well over half were actually born in Sussex or came from Sussex families; others were born elsewhere, but came to Sussex for various reasons and, by so doing, made their mark on the county.

Sussex is a fascinating county: running east to west, it is bordered by Kent, Surrey and Hampshire, and to the south by the sea – the county has a coastline that stretches for more than 68 miles (110 km) from Rye westwards to Bognor and Selsey Bill. It is often viewed as a rather genteel county, if not somewhat conservative: the focus is on the rolling downs, occasional cobbled streets, farmlands, forests and rivers, and on watering holes for the elderly, like Bexhill. But this can be a rather distorted view, for Sussex also contains raunchy and fashionable Brighton and bohemian Hastings, to name just two of its towns; and the county – to say nothing of its people – has a reputation for plain speaking, obstinacy (the ancient saying that Sussex people won't be 'druv') and rebelliousness.

Certainly the women included in this book display all those characteristics. From the 14th-century Lady Joan Pelham, who wrote a courteous letter to her absent husband while repelling an attack on Pevensey Castle, through to the 20th-century novelist Angela Carter, every woman here was either a rebel or an extremely strong-minded woman determined to put her own ideas into practice; in most cases, they were both.

Uncovering the stories of these women has not always been easy: some are well documented, but needed considerable research to reveal their Sussex connections; others are quite obscure, and only a passing reference provides a clue to their fascinating lives. It is quite shocking how many of the women, who were extremely important at the time, have fallen out of sight. Pioneer racing driver Dorothy (Dot) Levitt is one example. She raced in Brighton and Bexhill during the early 1900s and paved the way for later women racing drivers, but there are no local records of her achievements.

Looking through parish registers, walking through Sussex graveyards – and even flipping through older guidebooks, such as the Highways & Byways series published in the early years of the 20th century – provide tantalising glimpses of other individual women, not included in this book, who lived, worked and died in Sussex or who visited Sussex regularly. Either we know very little about them or their Sussex connections entailed more research than time permitted. For example, the Norwich poet and novelist Mrs Amelia Opie apparently went to Bognor every summer to visit and stay with the poet William Hayley; she left behind an extraordinary account of his daily habits and wrote the epitaph on his grave in Felpham.

Choosing the women for this book was not easy. The aim was to give as a wide a range as possible – hence the rather eclectic nature of the selection – and to provide as long a historical sweep as possible, so the earliest biography dates from the 14th century and the most recent come into the latter part of the 20th century. Perhaps Victorian women do get slightly more than their fair share, but they are particularly fascinating. The story of Sussex women is still far from over. The country continues to produce and attract amazing women: in fact, they read like a roll-call of achievement: Barbara Flynn, Jo Brand, Joanna Lumley, Dora Bryan (who was born in Lancashire, but adopted Brighton as her home town more than 30 years ago) and Annie Nightingale. Hastings and Brighton still generate determined women activists, such as Jo Wilding, whose sanction-busting visits to Iraq have made the news; and they inspire a wealth of women artists, such as Laetitia Yhap and Lorna Vahey. Only time will tell if they make the next generation of Sussex guidebooks.

THE
BIOGRAPHIES

Editor's Note

Each biography includes a short selective list of the subject's top works and places or things to see that are connected with her life. The Brighton & Hove Bus and Coach Company has a recent tradition of naming its buses after prominent local people (both men and women) and, where relevant, these are also mentioned, giving the ID number (rather than the route, which changes) of the bus in question.

VANESSA BELL
1879-1961

CHARLESTON, FIRLE

Vanessa Bell is one of the 'big names' linked with Sussex. She was a leading 20th-century artist and one of the first British artists to work in an abstract style. She will always be associated with the Bloomsbury set and with Charleston, the farmhouse near Firle.

Daughter of literary critic Sir Leslie Stephen, Vanessa was born in London. She had a sister Virginia (later Virginia Woolf, *see p.91*) and two brothers, Thoby and Adrian. Vanessa studied art and in 1901 became a student at the Royal Academy in London.

Following the deaths of their parents, Vanessa, Virginia and their two brothers moved to 46 Gordon Square in Bloomsbury. Free from constraints, they adopted an unconventional approach to life. In 1905 Vanessa founded the Friday Club to provide a venue for artists, and their house became the focal point for various writers, artists and intellectuals, including Lytton Strachey, Maynard Keynes, Leonard Woolf, Roger Fry and art critic Clive Bell, the notorious Bloomsbury set.

In 1906 Thoby died suddenly from typhoid fever; the following year Vanessa married Clive Bell. They had two sons, Julian and Quentin. Sexual freedom and open relationships were hallmarks of the Bloomsbury set, and in 1910 Roger Fry fell passionately in love with Vanessa and they had an affair. Until now Vanessa Bell's paintings had been fairly conventional, but – influenced by her husband and by Fry, who hosted the famous exhibition 'Manet and the Post-Impressionists' in London in 1910 – she began to adopt a bolder and more abstract approach. By 1914 she was painting in an entirely abstract style and producing decorative work for Fry's Omega Workshops.

By this time Vanessa had begun an affair with the artist Duncan Grant. Despite his homosexuality, they maintained a close and lifelong partnership, living and working together. They had a daughter, Angelica, but kept her paternity secret from her. Vanessa remained married to and friendly with Clive Bell, who brought Angelica up as his own daughter.

Vanessa was a pacifist, as were other members of the Bloomsbury set. When World War I broke out, she and her children, together with Duncan Grant and his then lover, David Garnett, left London for Sussex so that Grant could escape conscription. They rented Charleston Farmhouse, which was to be their country home for many years.

Vanessa and Duncan set up studios at Charleston and some of her finest work dates from this period. The two also decorated Charleston: over the years they painted walls, fireplaces and furniture in their distinctive post-Impressionist style. Fabrics, ceramics and screens from the Omega Workshops were incorporated into the decor, as were their paintings and those of their friends. Vanessa's paintings became more representational: she believed 'nature was more interesting' and painted still lifes, landscapes, interiors with figures and occasional portraits.

During the interwar years Vanessa based herself in London and exhibited frequently. She also travelled, but in 1939, with the outbreak of World War II, she returned to Charleston and a time of personal tragedy. Fry had died in 1934, Julian was killed in the Spanish Civil War and Virginia committed suicide in 1941. Vanessa was also estranged from Angelica, who by now knew her paternity. Her work fell out of favour, but she continued painting and living at Charleston until she died.

Vanessa Bell's Top Places

❯ Charleston Farmhouse, Firle: now renovated and managed by the Charleston Trust
❯ Berwick church: murals painted by Vanessa Bell and Duncan Grant
❯ Firle churchyard: burial place of Vanessa Bell and Duncan Grant
❯ National Gallery, London: portraits by Vanessa Bell of Virginia Woolf, 1912 and Aldous Huxley, 1929-30

Vanessa Bell's Top Works

❯ Studland Beach, 1916
❯ Interior with Two Women, 1932

CLEMENTINA MARIA BLACK
1853-1922

BRIGHTON

Clementina Black was a trade unionist, writer and suffragist. She was born in Brighton, one of six children. Her father, David Black, was a solicitor, town clerk and local coroner, who became an invalid when she was still a child. Her mother, Maria Patten, was a portrait painter who taught her at home. One of her sisters was Constance Garnett, later famous for translating Russian novels. Maria died in 1875, and Clementina, as the eldest daughter, was left to look after the family and her invalid father. She worked as a teacher in Brighton and began to write in her spare time, publishing her first novel, *A Sussex Idyll*, in 1877.

After her father's death, Clementina moved to Fitzroy Square in London. She continued writing, lectured on 18th-century literature and spent time in the British Museum researching social issues. In about 1886 she met and became friends with Eleanor Marx, daughter of Karl Marx, and through her became part of a circle of radicals, freethinkers and socialists who included Olive Schreiner and Beatrice Potter (later Webb) of the Fabian Society; it also included Amy Levy, a Jewish poet from Clementina's Brighton schooldays.

The late 1880s were a time of intense union activity and socialist ferment in Britain. Skilled workers such as engineers had unionised during the 1850s, but there was still a vast pool of unskilled labour working in dangerous, unprotected and exploitative conditions. Many, such as the dock workers, were striking for their rights; others, particularly those in the sweated industries, had no voice.

Clementina was determined to improve working conditions for women. It was not easy: there was still ambivalence about a woman's right to join a union and even about women working, particularly married women – many male workers saw women as a threat to their livelihood and some leading trade unionists argued that women should remain 'in their proper sphere' at home, instead of competing 'for their livelihood against the great and strong men of the world'. Clementina Black did not agree. In 1886 she became secretary of the Women's Protective and Provident League (WPPL), founded by Emma Patterson in 1874 and the first women's trade union. It represented dressmakers, upholsterers, artificial flower-makers, pickle workers and shopkeepers – all low-paid women's occupations, notoriously difficult to unionise.

In 1888 Clementina went as a delegate to the Trades Union Congress and called for equal pay for equal work – the first woman to do so publicly. She also spoke at the Fabian Society, describing the appalling and dangerous working conditions of low-paid women such as the match girls, and calling for the formation of a Consumers' League to boycott exploitative employers. Socialist Annie Besant was in the audience and, inspired by Clementina, decided to take matters further. With Clementina Black and others, she subsequently helped the match girls in their now-famous – and successful – strike.

Clementina resigned from the WPPL in 1889 and joined the Women's Trade Union League, helping to unionise women in London's East End. Five years later she helped to merge the League into a new organisation, the Women's Industrial Council (WIC). As president of the Council, she worked with other middle-class women, including Hilda Martindale and Cicely Corbett-Fisher (also a Sussex woman and the daughter of Marie Corbett, *see p. 31*), to assemble data on women's working conditions that could be used to lobby Parliament and force changes in the law to protect low-paid women workers. Their findings, which were based on 117 trades, were published in 1915 as *Married Women's Work*.

Clementina Black was especially concerned with the dreadful conditions of home workers and women in the sweated trades. Most were the wives or widows of casual labourers and were among the most vulnerable of workers. At a meeting of the Trades Union Congress in 1887, she passionately opposed a male trade unionist's motion to exclude women from the chain-making industry because it was too dangerous for women, by saying that although women did:

*suffer the physical evils [described]... there was not one injury that... could not
be capped by a worse story of the sufferings of women employed in trades which
no-one dreamed of forbidding, such as needlework and match-box making... But
men never proposed to interfere with these trades.Why?... Men did not work at
these trades and suffered nothing from the competition of women.*

A determined and popular woman, Clementina advocated a minimum
wage to prevent poverty and the formation of trade boards to protect
low-paid workers. She wrote two important books on the subject and
in 1909 the Trade Boards Act was passed, setting up trade boards to
protect workers in sweated industries.

She knew that women could not improve their situation until they
had the vote, and was active in the National Union of Women's Suffrage
Societies (NUWSS) editing its journal, *The Common Cause*, for a while.
She was one of the few women to meet Prime Minister Asquith in 1910
when the Conciliation Bill was discussed, which would have given limited
women's suffrage, although it was not passed.

She continued to write until increasing blindness prevented her, one
of her most successful novels being *The Agitator* (1894), which was highly
praised by Eleanor Marx. Clementina died in Surrey and is buried at
East Sheen cemetery. Like many women activists, she never married.
In 1890 she wrote a pamphlet, 'On Marriage', outlining her reasons:

*the strict letter of the law denies to the married woman the freedom of action
which more and more women are coming to regard not only as their just but also
as their dearest treasure, and this naturally causes a certain unwillingness on the
part of the thoughtful woman to marry.*

Clementina Maria Black's Top Places
- *58 Ship Street, Brighton: formerly the Black home*
- *Brighton bus, ID 658: Clementina Black*

Clementina Maria Black's Top Works
- *Sweated Industry and the Minimum Wage, 1907*
- *A Case for Trade Boards, 1909*
- *Married Women's Work, 1915*

LADY ANNE BLUNT
1837-1917

CRABBET PARK, NEAR CRAWLEY

A ccording to her obituary in *The Times*, Lady Anne Blunt was a 'distinguished and well-beloved personality', but outside racing circles her name is not perhaps as well known as it should be. She was a remarkable woman – an accomplished linguist, artist and horse-woman and a great Arabic scholar. With her husband, she was the first to bring Arabian horses into England and established a world-famous Arabian stud farm at her home, Crabbet Park in Sussex. Her achievements, however, are often overshadowed by or credited to her flamboyant and overbearing husband, Wilfred Blunt.

She was born Anne Isabelle Noel King on September 22nd 1837 in London and came from an illustrious family. Her grandfather was the poet Byron and her mother was Ada Lovelace, renowned for assisting Charles Babbage in the development of his 'analytical engine', the fore-runner of the computer. Her mother was caught up in her work with Babbage and died when Anne was 15, so she was brought up mainly by her grandmother, Lady Byron.

She was an attractive and intelligent child, with a 'gentle, old-fashioned dignity of manner' and a soft speaking voice. She was also a highly accomplished young woman: she studied drawing with John Ruskin and was an excellent artist – an architectural drawing that she did when she was 12 was hung in the Royal Academy, London. She was a competent violinist and owned two Stradivarius violins. As a young woman, Anne travelled extensively with her father and became fluent in French, German, Italian and Spanish. While staying in Florence she met Wilfred Scawen Blunt, an extremely handsome diplomat, poet – and woman-iser. The two married in 1869, when Anne was in her early thirties. By all accounts she was a thoughtful and self-effacing woman, but this disguised her undoubted determination, courage and resourcefulness. She was wealthy too, with an annual income of some £3,000, which must have appealed to her far less wealthy husband. In 1872 Blunt inherited the family estate at Crabbet Park, an old country house with some 4,000 acres (1,619 ha) of land. Lady Blunt redesigned and restored the house, which became their family home. To her lasting sorrow she experienced a number of miscarriages until, in 1873, she gave birth to a daughter, Judith, her only surviving child.

The Blunts shared a love of horses (Anne was an excellent horse-woman) and were both drawn to Arab culture. Blunt, who suffered from tuberculosis, needed hot, dry climates, so two months after Judith was born, and leaving the baby in England (some say with one of Blunt's former mistresses), they set out on the first of many journeys to Arabia and the Middle East. In 1875-6 they visited Egypt and then, travelling on horses and camels in the company of Bedouins, voyaged through the Sinai to Jerusalem. During the desert crossing they ran out of water and nearly died of thirst. Lady Blunt fell in love with the Bedouin culture and became a fluent Arabic speaker and writer. During the winter of 1878-9 she became the first-recorded woman to reach the Nejd, an inaccessible region in what is now Saudi Arabia. During her journeys she also crossed the Tigris and Euphrates Rivers, either on a goatskin raft or clinging to a swimming horse.

Lady Blunt was fascinated by Arabian horses, which she believed were the finest in the world. She feared they faced extinction and that to survive they needed to be bred in England. In 1877 she wrote in her diary: 'We have made a plan of importing some of the best Arazeh blood to England and breeding it pure there. It would be an interesting and useful thing to do.' In 1878 she sailed back to England, returning to Sussex with some Arabian stallions and six mares that would form the basis of the Crabbet Stud farm.

Over the years she bought more Arabian horses and shipped them back to Sussex, first directly from the Bedouins and subsequently from the great Egyptian horse breeder, Ali Pasha Sherif. She was an avid writer and kept detailed journals of her travels and horse-trading. Her journals not only display an extraordinary wealth of knowledge of horses and

Arab culture, but also reflect her keen scientific interest: she recorded every compass bearing and barometer reading. Her writings were later published and make fascinating reading, although apparently they were much edited by her husband.

Lady Blunt not only loved horses, but was an extremely able horse-woman. Wearing a Bedouin headdress and robe over stout English tweeds, she continued to ride until well into her late seventies and, according to her daughter, could still vault onto a horse unassisted when she was 77. She dislocated a knee on one of her desert journeys, but continued to ride for weeks supporting her swollen and useless leg in a rope tied to her waist.

By the early 1880s the Crabbet Stud farm had become world-famous. In 1882 the Blunts bought an estate outside Cairo, Sheykh Obeyd, where they founded a second stud. Lady Blunt divided her time between Egypt and Sussex, where she managed the stud and introduced different breeding programmes. Husband and wife drifted apart because of Blunt's constant infidelities, and in 1906 they finally separated when Blunt moved his current mistress into their home. The stud was divided, with Lady Blunt keeping half the horses and living at Crabbet Farm.

Egypt was, however, her great love and she spent her winters in Sheykh Obeyd. After 1915 she did not return to Sussex again and died in Cairo on December 15th 1917, honoured by her Arab friends as 'the noble lady of the horses'. The stud that she had founded continued until 1975 when a motorway was built through the Crabbet Estates. To this day most thoroughbred Arabians trace their heritage back to Crabbet.

Lady Anne Blunt's Top Places
◐ *Crabbet Park House, although there is little left of the stables and grounds*
◐ *Arab thoroughbred horses, most of which trace their ancestry to those Lady Blunt brought from the Middle East*

Lady Anne Blunt's Top Works
◐ *Bedouin Tribes of the Euphrates, 1879*
◐ *A Pilgrimage to the Nejd, 1881*
◐ *The Authentic Arabian Horse, 1945: completed by Lady Blunt's daughter, Lady Judith Wentworth*

BARBARA BODICHON
1827-91

WHATLINGTON

The mid-19th century saw the emergence of the first-ever organised women's movement in Britain, sometimes known as first-wave feminism. Small numbers of corseted, long-skirted and determined middle-class 'ladies' began to challenge Victorian sensibilities and convention and demand rights for women. The leading light, and by all accounts a remarkable powerhouse, was Barbara Bodichon, who during her long life was a feminist, social reformer, philanthropist and artist.

As Barbara Leigh Smith, she was born in Whatlington, near Battle. Her paternal grandfather had been active in the anti-slavery movement and her father, Benjamin Leigh Smith, was an enlightened and active man, who served as MP for Norwich and a magistrate in Hastings. Barbara's mother, Anne Longden, was a milliner and they had five children, of whom Barbara was the second eldest, although they never married. The reasons are unclear, but perhaps it was a protest against the forced dependence imposed on women through marriage. Either way, their unmarried status was considered scandalous, particularly by some of the Leigh Smiths, including Barbara's first cousin, Florence Nightingale.

Barbara spent most of her early life living in Pelham Crescent, Hastings. Her mother died when she was seven and her father brought up the family, dividing their time between Hastings and his London house. Believing that girls should have the same opportunities as boys, he provided a series of tutors who gave Barbara an excellent education. In 1848, when Barbara reached 21, her father gave her investments that brought in £300 a year, giving her an independence and freedom almost unheard of for women at that time. This enabled her to do exactly as she wished, and by 1849 she was studying art at the newly opened Bedford Ladies College, London.

Barbara's initial ambition was to be a professional artist. Her closest friend was poet and feminist, Bessie Rayner Parkes, and she also knew artist Mary Howitt, and Ann Samworth. She met some of the Pre-Raphaelites, helped to set up the Society for Female Artists, petitioned for the Royal Academy to accept women students and was a close friend of Gertrude Jekyll. She continued painting for most of her life, producing vivid landscapes of scenes in Britain and abroad.

She is best remembered, however, for her political work. A few women, such as Quaker Annie Knight, had begun to talk about the unthinkable – namely, votes for women – but Barbara was initially concerned to highlight and reform laws relating to women, particularly those to do with property. At that time, in the words of Sir William Blackstone, 'husband and wife are one and that is he'. Married women had virtually no legal status. On marriage, their property, goods and body became the property of their husbands; they did not even have rights over their own children. In 1854 Barbara Leigh Smith published *A Brief Summary in Plain Language of the Most Important Laws Concerning Women*, in which she pointed out how major laws concerning marriage, divorce and property discriminated against women.

The pamphlet was widely read and was used to lobby the Law Amendment Society with a view to reforming the laws. To this end, Barbara organised a back-up petition, obtaining 26,000 signatures in support of legal changes. With the help of male MPs, known to feminists as 'friends in the House', a Married Women's Property Bill was put before the House of Commons, but although a minor change was achieved, it came to a dead-end in favour of another reforming Bill to do with marriage and divorce. However, the wheels had been set in motion and, largely through Barbara's efforts, married women gained rights over their property in 1882.

Barbara now turned to women's work. By this time she had met and married a French doctor, Eugene Bodichon, who lived in Algiers. She had considered not marrying, but her new husband supported her feminist views and, in typically unconventional style, she spent the winter in Algiers with him and the remaining six months free and independent in England. She designed and built a house, Scalands Gate near Robertsbridge, where she entertained many friends, including the Rossettis and Marianne North (*see p. 70*). Gertrude Jekyll designed the garden.

The right to work was a major issue, particularly for middle-class women. While working-class women laboured long hours in factories and mills, their middle-class sisters suffered lives of enforced idleness. For them, marriage and motherhood were virtually the only acceptable professions. For Barbara Bodichon this state of affairs could not be allowed to continue. In a pamphlet, 'Women and Work', she stormed:

> *Fathers have no right to cast the burden of the support of their daughters on*
> *other men. It lowers the dignity of women and tends to prostitution, whether*
> *legal or in the streets… Adult women must not be supported by men if they are*
> *to stand as dignified, rational beings before God…Women must have work if*
> *they are to form equal unions.*

In 1859 Barbara and others set up the Society for the Promotion of Employment for Women in offices in Langham Place, London. Being a lowly governess was the only accepted paid occupation for single women of Barbara's class, so the 'Ladies of Langham Place' trained and encouraged women to seek work as printers, bookkeepers, clerks and shop assistants. They also set up the first business school for girls. Barbara took over a genteel newspaper, *The Englishwoman's Journal*, and, with Bessie Rayner Parkes, turned it into a campaigning mouthpiece, firing off articles on the situation of women, and demanding work and higher education for girls. No cause, if it improved the lot of women, was too insignificant. And, as Ray Strachey enthusiastically observed, at the heart of each new initiative was Barbara Bodichon, her 'golden hair and untiring enthusiasm' inspiring everyone around her.

In due course Barbara turned her attention to the cause of women's suffrage. Victorian feminists relied on male MPs to put their case in the House of Commons, and the most sympathetic was John Stuart Mill. Typically Barbara threw herself behind his election campaign, hiring a carriage plastered with posters and galloping around Westminster encouraging voters; and, despite or because of this, J.S. Mill was returned. Barbara Bodichon formed a committee and co-drafted a petition in support of women's suffrage, gathering nearly 1,500 women's signatures. She wrote and circulated pamphlets, thousands of which were printed, and another petition was circulated, collecting 3,000 or so signatures. But the time was not yet right: J.S. Mill's motion for female suffrage was defeated.

Barbara financed many projects close to her heart. She founded a progressive co-ed school in London, made funds available for a girls' college that later, in 1873, became Girton College, Cambridge, and took up philanthropic causes in and around Hastings. In 1877 Gertrude Jekyll designed a reading room at Scalands Gate that became an evening school for local men who were illiterate. Barbara became friends with, and promoted the work of, George Eliot, who, it is said, modelled her heroine Romola on her.

In 1877 Barbara Bodichon suffered a stroke that left her a semi-invalid. She died at Scalands Gate on June 11th 1891 and was buried in Brightling Church. She has never quite achieved the same fame as, say, the charismatic Pankhursts, which is a shame because she effectively founded the British women's movement, and women today owe her a great deal. In 2000 Hastings historian Helena Wojtczak celebrated Barbara's achievements by organising a blue plaque to commemorate them.

Barbara Bodichon's Top Places
◗ *9 Pelham Crescent, Hastings: blue plaque*
◗ *Scalands Folly, near Robertsbridge: formerly Scalands Gate*
◗ *Hastings Museum and Art Gallery: some of Barbara Bodichon's paintings, including The Pier Rocks (painted in Hastings) and Algerian landscapes*

Barbara Bodichon's Top Works
◗ *A Brief Summary in Plain Language of the Most Important Laws Concerning Women, 1854*
◗ *Married Women's Work, 1857*

LADY ANNIE BRASSEY
1839-87

HASTINGS

The Brassey name is well known in Hastings, usually because of Sir Thomas Brassey, a local benefactor who built and donated the Brassey Institute as a public library and art school. However, his wife, Lady Anna Brassey — or Annie, as she wrote her name — was also a leading light in Hastings society, as well as being the first woman to circumnavigate the globe in a yacht (albeit a highly luxurious one).

She was born Anna Allnutt, in London, the daughter of John Allnutt and Elizabeth Harriet. Her mother died while she was an infant and her grandfather and father brought her up. She loved country life and pursuits and, from an early age, showed a keen interest in botany.

In 1860, at St George's church, Hanover Square, she married Thomas Brassey (later Lord Brassey), eldest son of the wealthy railway contractor Thomas Brassey. The couple lived at Beauport Park, near Battle, then moved to Normanhurst Court, Catsfield, a splendid house built for them in 1870. The Brasseys also owned a house in London's Park Lane.

Like other women of her class, Annie (she became Lady Brassey in 1886) managed the house and estate at Normanhurst and did good works locally. She and her husband entertained lavishly: the artist Marianne North (*see p. 70*) recorded that the height of the winter season 1862-3 was a fancy ball held at Normanhurst Court. Annie supported her husband when he stood, successfully, as Liberal MP for Hastings in 1868 and, when a petition was lodged against him, she gave evidence in his favour, apparently showing 'great astuteness'.

Lord Brassey was an enthusiastic sailor, and although initially Annie suffered from seasickness, she soon became accustomed to life on board ship and sailed with her husband on his yacht in the Mediterranean and North America. A keen writer, she recorded every detail of their journeys, which were later published. Paintings show her as an elegant woman, writing a journal that is resting on her knee.

Following the success of these voyages, the Brasseys decided to embark on a round-the-world trip. Lord Brassey commissioned a fabulously luxurious yacht, which was equipped with three masts and a 340-horsepower steam engine. Carrying a crew of 32, plus the Brasseys' five children (all under 15), a nurse, lady's maid, the family pets and various friends, the *Sunbeam* set sail from England on July 1st 1876. It crossed the South Atlantic and passed through the Straits of Magellan into the Pacific, sailing on via Tahiti, Hawaii and Japan and then onwards to Ceylon, Aden and the Red Sea. When they reached the Suez Canal, Lady Brassey and her children disembarked to visit the pyramids, then travelled overland to rejoin the ship in Alexandria. She disembarked on other occasions to visit street markets in Rio, Valparaíso and Singapore and to explore the scenery in Tahiti, Ceylon and Hawaii.

Lady Brassey and her family arrived back at Hastings pier on May 27th 1877 to an enthusiastic reception. A committee had organised a 'welcome home' banquet for the Brasseys, which was held in the pier pavilion. *The Hastings and St Leonards Chronicle* devoted three and a half columns to the event, which was attended by 300 of the town's great and good (including the mayor), all of whom fêted the couple's achievements. The pier was decked out in bunting and dazzled with lights, the dining area was a mass of floral arrangements and the Queen's Hotel provided a 'stunning repast'. Musical entertainment was provided, including a song entitled 'Sunbeams', specially written for the occasion. During the after-dinner speeches Lord Brassey paid particular tribute to Annie, saying that the merit should be shared with his 'dear wife' and that had it not been for her wise counsel, he might have broken the journey at one point. Local dignitary Sir Kay-Shuttleworth complemented Lady Brassey on being a traveller, sailor, observer, writer and 'above all… an English yachtsman's wife and help-meet'. It was not appropriate, of course, for Lady Brassey to say anything in public.

In 1878 Annie published her account of their journey, entitled *A Voyage in the Sunbeam*. To her enormous surprise, it was an immediate success and brought her considerable fame. By 1898 her book had been through 19 editions and translated into several languages; in 1881 a cheap paper-covered edition was produced, one of the first examples of its kind. It is said that Prince Bismarck read her book, while smoking his evening pipe.

An avid collector, Lady Brassey returned to England from her voyages with numerous natural history and ethnological curios. She wanted the public to see these treasures and they were displayed in Hastings and in London, where her husband organised her collection as the Lady Brassey Museum in their Park Lane home. In 1919 much of the collection was donated to Hastings.

She continued her good works locally, particularly for the St John's Ambulance Association, but also continued to travel. In 1886 she left England for health reasons and went to India, Borneo and Australia, but became ill and died at sea, where she was buried.

Lady Annie Brassey's Top Places

◉ *Hastings Museum and Art Gallery, Bohemia Road: much of Lady Brassey's collection of artefacts*

◉ *Hastings Library, Claremont: formerly the Brassey Institute, designed by W.L. Vernon and donated to Hastings by Lord Thomas Brassey in 1887 to provide educational facilities for the community; it has a wonderful façade in Victorian Gothic style*

◉ *Catsfield: Lady Brassey's headstone*

Lady Annie Brassey's Top Works

◉ *The Flight of the Meteor, 1869*

◉ *A Cruise in the Eothen, 1872*

◉ *A Voyage in the Sunbeam, Our Home on the Ocean for Eleven Months, 1878*

CLARA ELLEN BUTT
1872-1936
SOUTHWICK

If any one singer could be said to encapsulate the spirit of an age, it would have to be Dame Clara Butt. She rose to fame at the time when English music was re-establishing itself in the concert hall after years of dominance by European composers, and the robust patriotism of composers such as Edward Elgar matched the mood of late Victorian and Edwardian society. Her booming contralto voice and magnificent stage presence, accentuated by her statuesque pro- portions and dramatic dress sense, suited the music perfectly, making her a favourite with audiences and one of the first real stars of the fledg- ling recording industry.

Born in Southwick, West Sussex, on February 1st 1872, Clara was the eldest daughter of Captain Henry Butt, a merchant seaman and oyster-dredger, and his wife Clara Hook, the great-granddaughter of the author Theodore Hook. Music-making was a popular pastime in middle-class families of the time, and her parents were both enthusias- tic amateur singers: they encouraged the young Clara to sing too, and soon recognised the richness and range of her voice. When the family moved to Bristol in 1880, her new headmistress also saw the potential of this remarkable voice and arranged for Clara to study with the conductor of the Bristol Festival Choir, Dan Rootham.

Thus began a long and successful career in music. Although she orig- inally trained as a soprano (and was capable of singing in that high register), it was the power of the lower end of her range that set Clara apart from other singers and convinced her that her true place was as a contralto. By the time she was 18 she had enough confidence in her voice to audition for a scholarship at London's Royal College of Music, and had the stature to match: she had grown to a height of more than 6 feet (1.8 m) – almost unheard of for a woman at that time. One of her audition pieces, John L. Hatton's song 'The Enchantress', included the line: 'Kings have trembled when I came, reading doom upon my face', which was delivered by the young Clara in the trombone-like contralto for which she became renowned. She later admitted, 'I don't know about the Kings, but those examiners, they certainly trembled!' Needless to say, she was immediately accepted as a student.

Whilst studying at the Royal College under Henry Blower, she was approached by Sir Joseph Barnby, who offered her the contralto solos in Arthur Sullivan's *The Golden Legend* with the Royal Choral Society at the Albert Hall. This performance in December 1892, along with a student production of Gluck's *Orfeo and Euridice* in which she took the role of Orfeo, established Clara as one of the finest singers of the time. Her interpretation of Orfeo was commended by the music correspondent of *The Times*, and the Prince of Wales arranged a repeat performance a few months later, the first of many occasions when she was to sing for members of the royal family.

While such an imposing height and 'port-wine' voice might be considered a figure of fun to a more sophisticated age, her contemporaries regarded Clara highly. Indeed, Queen Victoria herself commented that 'I have never liked the English language before, but in your mouth it is beautiful.' As her fame spread, she turned her attention to the songs and ballads that were so popular at the time, and to the stirring solo parts of oratorios such as Handel's *Messiah* and *Samson* and Elgar's *Dream of Gerontius*. After a period studying in Paris (partly paid for by the Queen), she soon established herself as a stalwart of the London concert scene and choral festivals throughout Britain.

In the hectic late 1890s Clara Butt teamed up with the baritone Robert Kennerley Rumford, with whom she toured North America in 1899. The following year they married in Bristol Cathedral, in a ceremony attended by many of the leading lights of the musical world and thousands of adoring fans; Arthur Sullivan composed an anthem for the service. This was the start of a long and successful marriage, but it did put an end to her operatic performances – Clara's new husband could not bear to have her involved in love scenes with other men; the only exception to this embargo on opera came in 1920, when she reprised her role as Orfeo, this time with Thomas Beecham as conductor and an all-female cast to which her 'Bertie' had no objections.

With the new century came new opportunities. Elgar had already written his song cycle *Sea Pictures* for her, and when his D major 'Pomp and Circumstance' march was first performed in 1901, Clara was greatly impressed; she asked if he could compose something similar for her to sing. 'You shall have that one, my dear,' came the reply, and words by A.C. Benson were added to the 'big tune' at the heart of the piece. The resulting song, 'Land of Hope and Glory', was dedicated to the coronation of Edward VII, but was forever associated with Clara Butt. It was an immediate success: demand for the sheet music and gramophone recordings almost outstripped supply. Her rousing rendering of this 'second national anthem' allegedly prompted Thomas Beecham to comment that her voice could be heard clear across the English Channel.

There then followed tours of most of the English-speaking world, which brought Clara increasing fame and fortune. Her concert performances became dramatic affairs, enhanced by her majestic outfits and, apparently, the first use of spotlights on the concert platform.

By this time she had transformed herself from an attractively statuesque young lady into an imposing and commanding performer. Audiences were treated to a spectacle as well as a musical experience – and on occasions a lecture of her opinions as a Christian Scientist, delivered in the masculine speaking voice that had led to some confusion when she used the telephone. She made much of the extensive range of her voice, both in pitch and intensity: although she was capable of a smooth transition from her light and sensitive upper register to the penetrating baritone boom for which she had become renowned, she more often than not accentuated the difference, leading one critic to comment, 'It is very apparent when she is changing gears.'

By the outbreak of World War I she was a very bankable performer, and put her talents to good use in a series of concerts in aid of the British

Red Cross Society and other war charities. In all, she managed to raise more than £100,000 during the course of the war, and it was no doubt for her charity work that George V made her a Dame of the British Empire in 1920.

It is tempting to imagine Clara Butt as a rather forbidding, humourless character, but there is much evidence to the contrary. She was well aware of her redoubtable, bellowing persona, and probably played to the gallery to some extent. Offstage, she enjoyed the opportunity to travel that touring gave her, and frequently visited the gaming tables of Monte Carlo – where she was affectionately known as 'La Grande'.

But it was not all plain sailing for Clara and Bertie. She was earning well (enough to finance her three sisters' singing tuition) and enjoying enormous success, but had her share of tragedy too. Her first son died of meningitis at school, and her second son committed suicide; then, in the 1920s, she developed cancer of the spine. All of this she bore with characteristic fortitude, continuing to work and even making some of her later recordings from a wheelchair. As late as 1933 she gave a recital in Sydney, Australia, which was attended by the young Joan Sutherland (later to become one of the world's leading contraltos), who never forgot the impact of that enormous voice and sensitive interpretation.

Dame Clara died at North Stoke in Oxfordshire on January 23rd 1936, within a few days of the deaths of Rudyard Kipling and George V. Some have said that the deaths of these three within such a short time of each other seems, in retrospect, to have foreshadowed the coming end of the British Empire. Happily for future generations, Clara Butt's voice has been preserved in numerous recordings.

Clara Ellen Butt's Top Works
- *Clara Butt, A Critical Survey: The Acoustic Years (CD: Marston 52029-2)*
- *Clara Butt (CD: Nimbus N17912)*

ANGELA CARTER
1940 - 1992

EASTBOURNE

Angela Carter's novels and short stories are fantastical master-pieces, shot through with eroticism, myth and violence. Considered one of the most innovative British writers of the late 20th century, Angela Carter is hard to place in the strait-laced conservatism of Eastbourne. But that is where she was born – at 12 Hyde Street – as Angela Olive Stalker.

As a child, she was sent to live with her grandmother in Yorkshire to escape wartime bombing. She remembered the period with great affection, later saying of her childhood that 'life passed at a languorous pace, everything was gently untidy, and none of the clocks ever told the right time'.

She rejoined her parents after the war and went to school in Balham, south London. She and her father often went to the cinema, which started her lifelong passion with films. Following school Angela worked for a while as a reporter on the *Croydon Advertiser*, a job that her father found for her, and then in 1960 married Paul Carter, an industrial chemist, and the couple moved to Bristol.

From 1962 to 1965 Angela read English at Bristol University. She also started writing, completing her first novel, *Shadow Dance*, during her second summer vacation; it was published in 1966. Two more novels followed: *The Magic Toyshop* (1967), one of her best-known books, and *Several Perceptions* (1967), for which she won the Somerset Maugham Award. In these novels she developed her trademark themes of sexual fantasy, myth and Freudian unconscious.

She separated from her husband and in 1970, using her award money, went to Japan for two years. Often short of money, she worked for a while as a bar hostess, an experience that she wrote about in *Fireworks* (1974) and in an essay entitled 'Poor butterfly'. Her experiences in Japan added exoticism and an obsession with violence to her writing style. She moved into macabre science fiction with her novels *Heroes and Villains* (1969), *The Infernal Desire Machines of Dr Hoffman* (1972) and *The Passion of New Eve* (1977). She also contributed regularly to *New Society* magazine, and published essays noted for their sadomasochistic content, in which women were raped, tortured and often murdered.

Angela Carter used fairy tales as the recurring theme for a collection of short stories published as *The Bloody Chamber* (1979). Often violent and erotic, they retold traditional fairy stories such as the legend of Bluebeard with a feminist slant. One of them, 'Company of Wolves', which was based on Little Red Riding Hood, was made into a successful film in 1984. In 1979 feminist publishing house Virago published *The Sadeian Woman and the Ideology of Pornography*. It had a mixed and stormy reception, with many feminists attacking the author for her sympathetic approach to de Sade.

By now Angela had met and was living with a potter, Mark Pearce, in south London. She held various university posts in Sheffield and East Anglia, and was writer-in-residence in the United States and Australia. Her novel *Nights at the Circus* was published in 1984, and told the story of Fevvers, a Cockney trapeze artist who grew wings; laden with symbolism, it established her as a novelist in the 'magic realism' school of writing, with Gabriel García Márquez and Salman Rushdie.

In 1983 Angela had a much-loved son, Alexander, with Mark Pearce. They married in 1991 around the time that she was diagnosed with lung cancer. Her last novel, *Wise Children*, was published in 1991 and she died on February 16th 1992, aged 51. Her friend, the novelist Salman Rushdie, wrote that 'English literature has lost its high sorceress, its benevolent witch queen'.

Angela Carter's Top Works

- *The Magic Toyshop, 1967*
- *The Bloody Chamber and Other Stories, 1979*
- *The Sadeian Woman, 1979*

MARIE CORBETT
1859-1932

DANEHILL

Marie Corbett was born in Kent, but on her marriage moved to Sussex, where she spent the rest of her life. She made an indelible mark on the county, campaigning for women's rights and rescuing children abandoned in the workhouse.

Born into a progressive Liberal family, Marie married Charles Corbett in 1881. He too was a Liberal and a lawyer. They made their home in Woodgate, a large house in the village of Danehill, and had a son and two daughters, Margery and Cicely. The area was highly conservative – in both senses of the word – and Marie soon shocked the gentry, both by cycling and by her political activities. According to Margery:

> My mother became an energetic cyclist, rebuked by her neighbours for showing inches of extremely pretty feet and ankles, regarded as highly indecorous. It was not only to the ankles that the neighbours objected. My parents were Liberals... as much hated and distrusted as Communists... and regarded as traitors to their class.

In 1869 the Municipal Franchise Act had given women ratepayers the right to vote in local elections; it also enabled women to serve as Poor Law Guardians. Marie seized the opportunities eagerly and became a member of the Board of Guardians for the Uckfield workhouse (one of the first women in Britain to hold such a position) and later the first woman to serve as a councillor on Uckfield District Council. Neither activity endeared her to the local gentry.

Marie Corbett was passionate about both local and national politics. She campaigned tirelessly for her husband, who was elected Liberal MP for East Grinstead in 1906, and co-founded the Liberal Women's Suffrage Society. She and Charles supported votes for women and, when the Liberal government refused to act, Marie threw herself into 'the cause' as an active member of Millicent Fawcett's National Union of Women's

Suffrage Societies (NUWSS). She was always a law-abiding suffragist rather than a militant suffragette. She co-founded the East Grinstead Suffrage Society (not that it attracted many members) and, with her daughters, was often seen in East Grinstead High Street calling for women's suffrage. It was a highly courageous step, given the amount of opposition she faced – and not just from men. According to a local survey, fewer than 20 per cent of women in East Grinstead supported votes for women. In 1913 Marie Corbett boldly organised a public meeting on votes for women. Some 1,500 people turned up to hear Marie and two other speakers, but mayhem broke out when youths started pelting them with eggs, tomatoes and stones. As the speakers ran for safety to a neighbouring house, the police stood by inactive, helping only when the mob began breaking into the house.

The women's vote was won in 1918, and from then on Marie devoted her time to her other great cause: helping children who had been abandoned in the workhouse. Focusing first on Uckfield, she sought out foster families for workhouse children, eventually managing to find homes for all the children. She visited the foster families regularly, and at one point was caring for at least 100 children locally. Having emptied Uckfield workhouse of children, she went on help those in Eastbourne, Brighton and London, similarly finding foster families for them. She continued with this work until she died, by which time she had found foster homes for some 500 children. In her obituary the *Mid-Sussex Times* commented that Danehill and the country were poorer for her death, describing her character as 'rare and beautiful'.

Marie Corbett's influence continued after her death through her daughters, Margery Corbett Ashby (1882-1981), who became president of the International Woman Suffrage Alliance, and Cicely Corbett-Fisher (1885-1959) who worked with Clementina Black (*see p.12*).

Marie Corbett's Top Places
- *Danehill*
- *East Grinstead: High Street*
- *Uckfield*
- *East Sussex Records Office, Lewes: records of Uckfield workhouse*

ELIZABETH DAVID
1913-1992

FOLKINGTON, NEAR POLEGATE

Britain's present-day preoccupation with food and cookery – especially exotic cuisine – stands in marked contrast to the situation in the first half of the 20th century. The change from a bland, unadventurous culinary tradition (apart from a few aristocratic gourmets) to a culture of exploration and experimentation in the kitchen was due to the pioneering work of cookery writers such as Elizabeth David. Her books on Mediterranean and continental food introduced the British public to regional recipes and made them available to ordinary people for the first time.

She was born in a 17th-century Sussex farmhouse, Wootton Manor in Folkington, the second of four daughters of Rupert Sackville Gwynne, Conservative MP for Eastbourne, and his wife, the Honourable Stella (née Ridley). Despite her privileged background, which included private tuition at home and a spell at St Clare's Private School for Ladies in Tunbridge Wells, Elizabeth's interest in food was awakened when her mother sent her to Paris to study art and French at the Sorbonne. After 16 years of unimaginative British cooking, her first taste of French cuisine was a revelation.

Her appetite for cooking was further aroused when she was given a copy of Hilda Leyel's *The Gentle Art of Cookery*, one of the few books then to describe exotic cuisine. Elizabeth later confessed that she would never have learned to cook, had she been given 'a standard Mrs Beeton instead of Mrs Leyel's wonderful recipes'.

Her love of the exotic and adventurous was not confined to food. She had early ambitions of becoming an actress and was attracted by the bohemian lifestyle that the theatre promised. After an affair with a married theatre director, and her failure to establish an acting career, she ran off with another married man, Charles Gibson-Cowan. Cowan's East End Jewish radicalism was in direct contrast to her conservative background and the attraction was irresistible. In 1939 the couple bought a boat and left England for Greece, but the outbreak of World War II interrupted their plans: they had to seek shelter in Antibes, where she met the writer Norman Douglas, who fast became her mentor with his love of all things Mediterranean. She and Cowan left Antibes in July 1940, but the Italians confiscated their boat and they were deported to Greece. Cowan then worked as a teacher on the island of Syros, which is where Elizabeth learnt the basics of Mediterranean cookery.

The German invasion of Greece in spring 1941 forced the lovers to flee once more, this time to Crete and then to Egypt. Elizabeth separated from Cowan in Alexandria, and for a time lived with a Sudanese chef in Cairo. There she met Anthony David, a lieutenant-colonel in the Indian army, and they married in August 1944. The couple moved to India at the end of the war, but illness forced Elizabeth to return to England, without her husband (or apparently any regrets), the following year. The marriage was always one of convenience, for Elizabeth at least, and when Anthony returned in 1947 their relationship was uneasy. They set up home in 24 Halsey Street, Chelsea, where Elizabeth lived for the rest of her life.

The return to England was difficult for her; the weather was cold, and because of rationing the food was even drabber than she remembered. To relieve the stultifying effect this was having on her, after seven years of travelling abroad, Elizabeth David started writing about the food she had learnt to love. A friend working for the magazine *Harper's Bazaar* suggested she write a regular cookery column, and the success of her articles culminated in the publication of *A Book of Mediterranean Food* in 1950, followed the next year by *French Country Cooking*.

Throughout the 1950s she continued to produce books, many of them extensively researched on trips to Italy and France. She moved from *Harper's* to *Vogue* magazine, and wrote articles for several national newspapers, changing the culinary habits of the nation. Her writing style was readable and witty, and her no-nonsense approach even to complex recipes was inspirational.

Her private life was not so successful. A long-standing affair with Peter Higgins, whom she had met in Cairo, led to the break-up of her marriage and eventual divorce in 1960. But the affair did not last either, and Elizabeth David slipped into depression fuelled by overwork, alcohol and sleeping pills. In 1963 she suffered a stroke, which cruelly impaired her sense of taste, and she virtually gave up writing.

But Elizabeth could not stay away from the world of cookery for long, and in 1965 with four other partners she set up a kitchenware shop in Pimlico – the first of its kind. Its success was assured by the name Elizabeth David Ltd, and the enterprise inspired her to resume writing: at first booklets for the shop and then full-length books. Unfortunately she was not as good a businesswoman as she was a writer, and she and her partners fell out and she left the business in 1973, although it retained her name.

The return to full-time writing in the 1970s produced some of her finest books, but she was no longer able to work at the feverish pace she had managed 20 years previously. She was further hampered by injuries from a car accident in 1977, which marked the beginning of a period of failing health. She had a further two cerebral haemorrhages in her late seventies, and died at her Halsey Street home in 1992.

Elizabeth David was buried at St Peter's church, Folkington. Her life was celebrated at a service in St Martin-in-the Fields, London, and a 'memorial picnic' took place at the Institute of Contemporary Arts. In 2006 the BBC showed a docudrama on Elizabeth David entitled *A Charming Monster*.

Elizabeth David's Top Place

◗ *St Peter's church, Folkington: Elizabeth David's headstone*

Elizabeth David's Top Works

◗ *Mediterranean Food, 1950*
◗ *French Country Cooking, 1951*
◗ *Italian Food, 1954*
◗ *French Provincial Cooking, 1960*

CHRISTIANA EDMUNDS
1827-1905
BRIGHTON

E legant and middle-class, Christiana Edmunds achieved notoriety
as 'The Brighton Poisoner'. She was born in Margate, but took
lodgings at 16 Gloucester Street, Brighton with her mother after
her father's early death. There she encountered a local doctor, Dr Beard.
He was married with children, but Ms Edmunds fell in love with him,
became acquainted with his wife and bombarded him with passionate
love letters.

Feeling perhaps that the only obstacle in her way was Mrs Beard,
Christiana set out to poison her. She called on Mrs Beard bearing a box
of strychnine-laced chocolates as a gift. Mrs Beard bit into one, but spat
it out complaining of a disgusting taste, at which Ms Edmunds promptly
left, taking the chocolates with her. Mrs Beard became ill, but recov-
ered. Her husband was suspicious, but instead of approaching the police,
accused Christiana Edmunds of attempted murder and banned her from
his house.

Christiana now embarked on a highly convoluted plan to switch suspi-
cion away from her and onto the confectioners, J.G. Maynard's of 39-41
West Street, Brighton. Claiming that she needed strychnine to poison
some cats, she bought it from a chemist, Isaac Garrett, of 10 Queen's
Road. She then paid small boys to buy chocolate creams on her behalf,
took the chocolates home, carefully injected strychnine into them, then
told the boys to return them to Maynard's, in exchange for smaller ones.
Quite unconsciously Mr Maynard began selling poisoned chocolates to
all and sundry. Mysteriously, several people became ill, and in June 1871
a four-year-old boy, Sidney Albert Barker, on holiday with his parents,
died after eating a chocolate cream purchased at Maynard's. An inquest
was held into the boy's death, at which Christiana Edmunds gave
evidence, claiming that she knew of several people who had become ill

after eating chocolates from Maynard's. Not surprisingly, the confectioner denied any wrongdoing. A verdict of accidental death was returned, but the local press seized on the case, and the elegant Christiana became a local celebrity, particularly after she accused the police of stupidity for failing to realise there was a poisoner at large.

She now intensified her campaign in a most bizarre way, sending anonymous poisoned food parcels to prominent Brighton residents, many of whom became ill. Press interest intensified, the people of Brighton panicked, and the police offered a reward for information. Finally Dr Beard went to the police with his suspicions, as did the chemist who had sold the strychnine. Christiana Edmunds was arrested and charged with murder. Evidence against her grew as statements were taken from Dr Beard, the chemist and the boys. The public was fascinated and the case became such a cause célèbre that hearings were moved from Lewes to the Old Bailey in London. The public's interest was fuelled even further when Mrs Edmunds took the stand to reveal that there was a long history of insanity in the family: Christiana's father and brother had both died in asylums and her sister had attempted suicide.

In a last-ditch attempt to save herself, Christiana Edmunds told the court she was pregnant by Dr Beard. Examination proved this was not the case and she was sentenced to death. Brighton newspapers were delighted, but opinions in the national press were divided: *The Times* accused her of a 'vicious' crime and of acting with 'cold-blooded indifference' to 'scatter death throughout the town…' *The Daily Telegraph* said she was 'a wretched, half-crazed creature, the sister, daughter and grandchild of lunatics' and claimed that hanging her would be disgraceful.

Following appeals to the Home Secretary and Queen Victoria, the sentence was commuted and Ms Edmunds was sent to Broadmoor, where she died aged 78. But she continues to fascinate, and in March 2006 was the subject of one of the BBC's Saturday radio plays.

Christiana Edmunds' Top Places
◉ *16 Gloucester Place, Brighton: home of Christiana Edmunds and her mother*
◉ *10 Queen's Road, Brighton: formerly Isaac Garrett, Chemist*

MARIA ANNE FITZHERBERT
1756 - 1837

BRIGHTON

Mrs Fitzherbert was the secret wife of the Prince Regent, later George IV. A striking and flamboyant woman, she was painted by Gainsborough and Reynolds and became the talk of fashionable society.

Her father was Walter Smythe, a soldier, and her mother was Mary Errington. In 1775 Maria married Edward Weld, a Staffordshire landowner, who died three months later. She remarried in 1778, her second husband being Thomas Fitzherbert, whose name she always kept. He too died in 1781, leaving her a wealthy widow with an annual allowance of £2,000 and their London house; after a suitable period of mourning Maria re-entered society, attending the London and Brighton seasons.

Mrs Fitzherbert claimed she first met the Prince of Wales in Chiswick in 1780 when she was driving with her husband in their carriage. She met him again at the opera in 1784, and he soon became completely infatuated and pursued her relentlessly. As a devout Catholic, however, she refused to become his mistress and made plans to leave for Europe. The Prince made a dramatic suicide attempt and she agreed to marry him on her return. She accepted a ring – apparently something she regretted – and in October 1785 returned to England to honour her decision.

The Prince and Mrs Fitzherbert were married in secret in December 1785. Reverend Robert Burt conducted the ceremony in her drawing room, and the witnesses included one of Mrs Fitzherbert's brothers. The Prince wrote out the marriage certificate, but the marriage was illegal: the Acts of Settlement (1701) and of Union (1707) forbade an heir to the throne from marrying a Catholic, and under the Royal Marriages Act (1772) the King's permission was needed.

Despite this, the couple honeymooned together and although they maintained separate establishments, were often seen together. Their relationship and 'marriage' soon became common knowledge. Initially fashionable society shunned Mrs Fitzherbert, who closed up her London house and went to Brighton, where she rented a small villa near to the Marine Pavilion. The Prince later bought her a house at 54 The Steine.

The marriage became the talk of the town, and Mrs Fitzherbert's situation in relation to the Prince was even discussed in the House of Commons. She broke off the relationship, but after the Prince made a second suicide attempt she relented again, despite being ridiculed and caricatured. The relationship was stormy: the Prince was an inveterate womaniser and had many affairs, although he always returned to Mrs Fitzherbert. He was, however, seriously in debt and in 1795 married his cousin, Caroline of Brunswick. The Prince was unhappy and con- tinued to court Mrs Fitzherbert. Being assured by the Pope that her marriage was valid, she agreed to a reconciliation with him in 1799. Their relationship continued for some time until finally Mrs Fitzherbert lost patience with the Prince's infidelities. They made a final break in 1811, after which they saw very little of each other. The Prince contin- ued to pay Mrs Fitzherbert a substantial annuity and when he died, in 1830, he was wearing a miniature of her around his neck, which was buried with him.

Mrs Fitzherbert continued to live in Brighton. By now public opinion had switched in her favour and she was, as the essayist John Wilson Croker observed, treated like royalty until her death:

> They don't quite Highness her... but they Madam her prodigiously, and
> stand up longer for her arrival than for ordinary folks... and go as near to
> acknowledging her for Princess as they can, without actually giving her the title.

Maria Anne Fitzherbert's Top Places
- Old Steine, Brighton: Mrs Fitzherbert's villa (now the YMCA)
- St John's Baptist church, Kemp Town: blue plaque
- Brighton bus, ID 805: Maria Fitzherbert

MARY ANN GILBERT
1776 - 1845

EASTBOURNE

Mary Ann Gilbert, a member of the wealthy and prestigious Gilbert family who have owned land in and around Eastbourne since the mid-17th century, should perhaps be seen as a role model for those who advocate the benefits of self-sufficiency. Or she may just have been a paternalistic landlord. Either way, during the 1830s she set out on a practical and moral mission to resolve the problem of rural poverty and restore independence to the landless poor, through an innovatory allotment system that she introduced around Beachy Head.

The 1830s were a period of great hardship among rural labourers: in 1830-1 the Swing Riots reached their height in Sussex, with an outburst of rick-burning as the landless poor protested against their dreadful conditions. Some relief was available through the parishes, but poverty, hunger and humiliation were the order of the day. For most parish authorities, the unemployed were feckless, idle, lazy and work-shy; they would rather subsist on meagre handouts from the parish than work.

Mary Ann Gilbert disagreed completely. She believed the poor – or paupers as they were known – would much rather support themselves through productive work than be demoralised and humiliated through the Poor Rate, which she 'would rather see… sunk in the sea than employed as now to the misery and moral deterioration of my fellow creatures'. A practical and rational woman, she not only believed that useful work would redeem the poor, but also that if the poor could support themselves through productive work, this would ease the burden on parish poor relief. Two problems solved at a stroke: little wonder that the social reformer Edwin Chadwick supported her ideas.

To this end, she set up a pilot scheme to cultivate wasteland near Beachy Head, land that she had inherited from her father and owned jointly with her husband, Davies Gilbert. She employed paupers to remove soil and clay from nearby marshland, transport it to the waste-land (which she called 'the beach') and take flint pebbles back to the marshland to replace the soil. Her scheme worked: she employed 27 paupers, purchased and drained marshland and brought wasteland under cultivation. The paupers also produced a healthy crop of potatoes from the newly cultivated land and, seeing the possibilities, were keen to rent land from Mrs Gilbert.

In 1832 Mary Ann sent a preliminary report on the success of her scheme to Dr Whately, Archbishop of Dublin, who had advised her on land reclamation. She decided to extend her scheme and, within a short period, nearly 200 paupers (some with families) were renting allot-ment-sized parcels of land from Mrs Gilbert and growing potatoes, turnips and mangelwurzels; some were also keeping cows and pigs on the allotments. To Mrs Gilbert's delight and vindication, the paupers were managing to pay their rent through their own hard work.

Despite the obvious success of her scheme, Mrs Gilbert had to provide evidence to the local parish officials. She did detailed and complex calcu-lations proving that the cost of reclaiming and working land was cheaper than parish relief, and sent out a wealth of reports, letters and papers about her scheme, even sending some potatoes from the allotments to Lord Liverpool to emphasise her point. He did not share her faith in Sussex labourers, claiming that they drew more heavily on poor relief than labourers elsewhere. Mrs Gilbert hotly disputed this, saying that when she asked local labourers whether they wanted to emigrate – a Petworth emigration project was under way at the time – they replied, 'There is America in England.' She also claimed:

> There is far more intelligence amongst labourers than those suppose who have
> not questioned them, they eagerly read the papers in hopes of the proposed Poor
> Law Amendment and say they believe the government has forgotten them.

Mrs Gilbert became a member of the Labourers' Friend Society, which shared her aims, and remained certain that the way to resolve rural poverty was to rent out land at a fair price to unemployed farm workers; the land needed to be of a size that could be worked with a spade, rather than a plough. Some of the opposition to Mrs Gilbert's scheme was that if the landless poor rented larger areas of land, they would become too independent and no longer available for seasonal casual work.

Mary Ann Gilbert believed passionately that the poor wanted work, not handouts. She loaned money to her tenants so that they could buy cows or pigs and frequently recorded that all loans were paid back. After a while she managed to convince others, bombarding Sussex men of influence with her findings. In 1835 Poor Law Guardians in 14 Sussex parishes, from Seaford to Pevensey, met in Eastbourne and recorded their findings that the poor were thankful for the work and it was cheaper to use men with handcarts than cattle-drawn ploughs; they also agreed to subsidise the venture.

Very much a product of her time, Mrs Gilbert set out to educate the poor morally. An iron gateway – the first of its kind in Sussex – led into the allotments and on it was a sign proclaiming: 'Here waste not Time and you'll not want Food.' She also presented every allotment tenant with a printed card pointing out that the price of two glasses of gin a day over a year would pay for:

- ✧ *a man's shirt*
- ✧ *a pair of men's stockings*
- ✧ *a pair of women's stockings*
- ✧ *a shift and muslin cap*
- ✧ *a printed cotton gown*

- ✧ *a man's cotton shirt*
- ✧ *a man's fustian coat*
- ✧ *a pair of blankets*
- ✧ *a neck handkerchief*
- ✧ *a pair of men's shoes*
- ✧ *a pair of women's shoes*

- ✧ *a flannel petticoat*
- ✧ *a coarse cloth cloak*
- ✧ *a quilted waistcoat*
- ✧ *fustian trousers, lined*
- ✧ *a pair of cotton sheets*

She also advocated ways of improving husbandry. These included installing water butts to catch rainwater; dibbling rather than broadcasting wheat; stacking wheat in haystacks on stone piles rather than storing it; stall-feeding cows; forking soil; and conserving liquid manure for fertiliser. She insisted these methods should be used on the allotments, stating that tenants would be evicted otherwise. Not everyone agreed with her methods, but the Eastbourne workhouse installed their own water butt, which provided water for more than 150 inmates.

Mrs Gilbert's allotment scheme was highly successful: in 1830 she had some 50 allotment tenants, and by 1835 there were 213, nearly all of whom were managing to pay their rent through their crops. The Labourers' Friend Society commented that the scheme meant a poor man 'gives to his country, by thus giving to his family, a considerable income, he saves to his country, by not becoming burdensome, another considerable increase…' And a paper Mrs Gilbert wrote on her allotment scheme was read to the Highland Agricultural Society in Edinburgh in 1844.

In the 1840s she went further, founding two agricultural schools, one at Willingdon and the other at East Dean. They too were self-supporting and encapsulated all of her ideas. Teachers did not receive a salary, but were paid a small weekly amount by each pupil. The schools, which were for designed for the children of allotment tenants, taught reading, writing, account keeping, Bible studies and husbandry. Each school had its own water butt and cow stalls.

Mary Ann Gilbert died in 1845, having also found time to have eight children, one of whom, John Davies Gilbert, played a significant role in developing Eastbourne. On her death the *Sussex Advertiser* stated:

> Mrs Gilbert by her industrial schools and by locating a family on a given small area of land… managed to prove the error of supporting the pauper population… in idleness and of their continuing to be mere consumers when they might be much better employed as producers of wealth.

She had her critics. The political economist John Stuart Mill believed that allotments were a way of 'making people grow their own poor rate' and that, with full employment and good wages, they would be unnecessary. Interestingly, during the two world wars the allotments once again proved their worth.

Mary Ann Gilbert's Top Places
- *Whitbread Hollow Allotments: the area of land between Cow Gap and Eastbourne (now covered by sports pitches) was formerly the allotment site*
- *Sussex Archives: papers of the Gilbert family*

MARTHA GUNN
1726 - 1815

BRIGHTON

Sea bathing in Brighton took off in the early 1750s when Lewes doctor Richard Russell published a treatise on its highly beneficial and therapeutic effects. People flooded into Brighton, transforming the once-sleepy fishing village into a highly fashionable resort, aided by the arrival, in the 1780s, of the Prince Regent, the Prince of Wales.

But sea bathing then was not as straightforward as it is today. It involved modestly descending from a cumbersome bathing machine into the waves, assisted by so-called 'dippers' (for women) and 'bathers' (for men). Martha Gunn was the unchallenged 'queen' of the Brighton dippers. For more than 60 years she assisted countless women bathers into the sea and became one of the best-known Brighton characters of her time.

Virtually nothing is known of Martha's early life, but she was probably from one of the local fishing families, many of whom worked as dippers or bathers from about 1750. Martha Gunn, however, was the best known; she was said to be a strong, rotund woman and certainly needed to be, because dipping was strenuous work.

She started her working day at six in the morning, positioning herself near the bathing machines that were lined up on the foreshore. The machines were large wooden hut-like structures mounted on wheels. Would-be bathers entered the machines, where they removed corsets and petticoats and prepared themselves for bathing. A horse dragged the machine into the water and then Martha, like the other dippers, helped to turn it around, so that the bather could descend from the back of the machine down some steps into the sea. At this point Martha would grip the bather's arms and immerse or dip her into the waves, holding the woman's head underwater if the sea was calm. According to the medics, three immersions or dips were needed for maximum benefit.

Having dipped one woman, Martha then helped her back into the machine and prepared to repeat the whole performance many times during the course of a day. Rain or shine, calm or storm, Martha Gunn did this work year in, year out, standing all day in the sea. She soon became a well-known figure on Brighton beach and there are various accounts of her at work. In 1806 the *Morning Herald* described a typical morning:

> The Beach this morning was thronged with ladies, all anxious to make interest for a dip. The machines, of course, were in very great request, though none could be run into the ocean in consequence of the heavy swell, but remained stationary at the water's edge, from which Martha Gunn and her robust female assistants took their fair charges, closely enveloped in their partly coloured dresses, and gently held them to the breakers, which not quite so gently passed over them.

Dipping was a paid profession, and Martha dipped genteel ladies of all ranks and ages. She was highly respected and, according to some sources, was said even to have dipped the Prince of Wales himself – although this is debatable, because men and women were strictly segregated on the beach. She was, however, a great favourite with the Prince of Wales and had access to the kitchens at the Pavilion, where she was sometimes given food. It is said that on one occasion she either took or was given some butter, which she hid in her pocket when the Prince of Wales suddenly entered the kitchen. For some reason the Prince decided to keep her talking in the kitchen, while gradually nudging her towards the cooking range; not surprisingly, the butter melted and dripped down her clothes.

Martha Gunn's fame was recorded in paintings, cartoons and etchings, most of which showed her as a substantial woman, dressed in a voluminous bonnet, wearing an apron over her clothes to protect her from the sea water. The Prince of Wales commissioned a portrait of her, which was painted by John Russell (1745-1806) and hangs today in the Royal Pavilion. One cartoon shows her with a large broom sweeping away the invading French from the coast, and poems were written about her. According to one anonymous poet (obviously male), there were plenty of dippers, but:

> The King of them all is 'Old Smoaker',
>> The Queen of 'em 'Old Martha Gunn'.
> The ladies walk out in the morn,
>> To taste of the salt-water breeze,
> They ask if the water is warm,
>> Says Martha, 'Yes, Ma'am, if you please,'
> Then away to the machines they run
>> Tis surprising how soon they get stripped;
> I oft wish myself Martha Gunn,
>> Just to see the young ladies get dipped.

Martha continued working until she was well into her eighties, although ill health eventually meant that she no longer took bathers into the water. Not long before her death, she told an author she no longer bathed because:

> I a'nt so strong as I used to be, so I superintend on the beach… while I've health and life, I must be bustling amongst my old friends… I think I ought to be proud, for I've as many bows from man, woman, and child, as the Prince hisself; aye, I do believe, the very dogs in the town know me.

Martha Gunn died, aged 88, in Brighton. A huge crowd turned out to watch her funeral procession and she was buried in the churchyard of St Nicholas. Her house at East Street still survives, and there is a pub in Brighton named after her. The profession of dipping itself died out in about the 1850s.

Martha Gunn's Top Places
- 34 or 36 East Street (sources disagree), Brighton: Martha Gunn's house
- Royal Pavilion, Brighton: portrait of Martha
- St Nicholas's churchyard, Brighton: her headstone
- Upper Lewes Road, Brighton: Martha Gunn pub
- Brighton bus, ID 806: Martha Gunn

PHOEBE HESSEL

1713-1821

BRIGHTON

Brighton attracts colourful characters, and none more so than Phoebe Hessel, cross-dressing soldier and centenarian. According to her tombstone, she:

> *served for many years as a private soldier in the 5th Regiment of foot in different parts of Europe and in 1745 fought under the command of the Duke of Cumberland at the battle of Fontenoy, where she received a bayonet wound in her arm.*

To this day the British army does not allow women to serve on the battle-field, but there are plenty of stories of women who dressed up as men to enlist. Phoebe Hessel is one of the best known, although details of her life are conflicting. She was born in Stepney, London, as confirmed by baptismal records in St Dunstan's church. Apparently her father was a soldier and, according to one version, after her mother's death he taught her to play the fife and drum and took her with him, disguised as a boy, to serve in the army. It is said that she served in the infantry for about 17 years, seeing active service in the Caribbean and on mainland Europe, where she was wounded at the Battle of Fontenoy. No one appears to have recognised her as a woman.

According to another and perhaps more romantic version, in 1728, when Phoebe was 15, she disguised herself as a man and enlisted in the army to accompany her lover, a soldier called Samuel Golding. In this version, too, she served in the army for 17 or 18 years without anyone realising she was a woman. In later years, when asked how she had been able to keep her secret for so long, she claimed that when it became too much for her, she dug a hole in the ground and confided her secret to the earth. Eventually her lover was wounded, discharged from the army and sent to a hospital in Plymouth. Phoebe finally confided her secret to the general's wife, and was discharged from the army to join Golding, whom she married. The couple lived in Plymouth for 20 years, and Phoebe had nine children, only one of whom survived (but later perished at sea).

After her husband's death Phoebe moved to Brighton – then a small fishing village – where she married a Mr Hessel (either Thomas or William). He died when she was about 80; she received three guineas from the parish, bought herself a donkey and earnt a living selling vegetables and fish in and around Brighton. Decked out in a brown serge dress, white apron and hooded black cloak, and walking with a thick oak stick, she became a well-known figure in Brighton and lived to a ripe old age, telling anyone who cared to listen about her army exploits.

Phoebe Hessel came to the attention of the Prince Regent, who was intrigued by her and in 1808, hearing that she had fallen on hard times and was in the workhouse, granted her a pension of half a guinea a week. She left the workhouse and, although now in her nineties, went back to selling her wares – gingerbread and oranges – on the corner of Marine Parade and Old Steine. Her reputation grew, people stopped constantly to talk to her, and she observed and heard everything going on around her. It is said that she overheard the notorious highwayman James Rooke talking about his part in a robbery and shopped him to the police, leading to his arrest and public hanging.

Phoebe remained a favourite of the Prince Regent and, when he succeeded to the throne in 1820, as George IV, he invited her to attend the coronation celebrations in Brighton. She died on December 12th 1821, aged 108. A local pawnbroker paid for her gravestone, which was later restored by the Northumberland Fusiliers, who (whether accurately or not) considered her part of the regiment.

Phoebe Hessel's Top Places

❂ St Nicholas's churchyard, Brighton: Phoebe Hessel's gravestone

❂ Old Steine, Brighton

❂ Brighton bus, ID 807: Phoebe Hessel

SOPHIA JEX-BLAKE
1840-1912

HASTINGS

Hastings has produced many pioneering women, not least Sophia Jex-Blake, whose determined efforts against formidable odds helped to open up the male-dominated medical profession to women.

She was born at 3 Croft Place (now 16 Croft Road), Hastings, where she spent the first years of her life. When she was 11, the family – her father, Thomas Jex-Blake, was proctor of Doctors' Commons – moved to 13 Sussex Square, Kemp Town, Brighton. She was educated at home and at a series of boarding schools: she was a bright child, although 'stormy, tumultuous and unmanageable' – traits that always stayed with her.

By the time she was 17 Sophia had decided to be a teacher and, despite opposition from her father, she went to Queen's College for Women, which had been founded in 1847. She was a skilled mathematician and went on to tutor in maths at Queen's College, although her father, considering it an inappropriate activity for a woman, insisted she should not receive a salary. While at the college she met future activists Octavia Hill and Elizabeth Garrett, who was the first woman to qualify as a doctor in Britain.

In 1862 Sophia went to Germany where she taught for a year, and then to the United States to observe teaching methods in Boston. There she met Dr Lucy Sewall, resident physician at the New England Hospital for Woman and Children. They became lifelong friends. She started studying at the New York Infirmary for Women in New York, but her father died and she returned to England.

Sophia started looking for somewhere to study medicine in Britain, which was not an easy matter. Women were not welcome in the medical profession, other than as midwives, and under the Medical Act of 1858 could not be medical students or qualify as doctors. If they qualified abroad, where medical schools were more welcoming, their qualifications were not recognised. Not one to let this stand in her way, in 1869 Sophia Jex-Blake began what Ray Strachey described as 'her assault upon the entrenched fortress of the medical profession' – it turned out to be an awfully long assault.

She chose Edinburgh University, but immediately met opposition: the university would accept her, but would certainly not tutor male and female students together – far too indelicate – nor would they provide separate classes for one woman, even though Sophia Jex-Blake was paying. Teaming up with four other like-minded women, Sophia managed to organise classes for them. They began their studies, but hostility to their presence from the university senate and male students was overwhelming. The group was constantly harassed and in 1870 male students organised a protest, later known as the 'Riot at Surgeons Hall'. As the women approached the hall for an anatomy demonstration, a mob of nearly 200 male students prevented access, jeering and throwing mud. According to the *Edinburgh Courant*:

> The appearance of the ladies was greeted with a howl, which might have made those who are supposed to be possessed of more temerity, quail, but it seemingly had no effect on the ladies, for they most unconcernedly advanced towards the gate.

The women gained access, but all was chaos, exacerbated when the men let a sheep into the hall. Apparently the infuriated professor suggested it should stay because it had more sense than those who sent it.

Sophia Jex-Blake had already been firing off articles to the press, university authorities and prominent people in the medical profession, but the riot aroused major public interest and some sympathy. Opinions were sharply divided on the question of women doctors. Many eminent people were absolutely opposed, claiming that medicine was an inappropriate profession for women and that female doctors were not necessary. Some considered that women were not equal to the gruelling challenges of medicine and would fail. In response, Sophia Jex-Blake fired off one of her many angry letters to *The Lancet*, saying:

> State clearly what attainments you consider necessary for a medical practitioner … put no obstacles in our way… subject us ultimately to exactly the same ordinary examinations and tests, and if we fail to acquit ourselves… reject us; if, on the contrary… we reach your standards, and fulfil all your requirements … give us then the ordinary medical licence or diploma and leave the question of our ultimate success or failure … to be decided by ourselves and the public.

Sophia's campaigning took its toll and she failed her final exams in 1873. But by now Edinburgh refused to allow the women to graduate, whether or not they completed – a decision upheld by a panel of judges. Sophia left Edinburgh, went to London and from 1874 channelled her energies into campaigning for new laws to allow women to qualify as doctors. With Elizabeth Garrett and others, she founded the London School of Medicine for Women in Brunswick Square to train women and, hopefully, affiliate to a major hospital for clinical experience.

Her high-profile campaigning achieved partial success in 1876 when Parliament passed a law permitting examining bodies to accept women candidates. Sophia Jex-Blake qualified in 1877, first at Berne University, then Dublin, becoming the fifth woman on the Medical Register.

In 1878 Sophia Jex-Blake opened a dispensary and medical school for women in Edinburgh, and in 1885 Edinburgh University finally accepted women medical students. In 1887 she founded the Edinburgh School of Medicine for Women and in 1899 retired and moved back to Sussex, to a cottage, Windydene, in Mark Cross, where she died aged 72. She never married, apparently once saying, 'I love women too much to ever love a man', but had a long-term companion, Dr Margaret Todd. She and Margaret were buried at Rotherfield Church.

Sophia Jex-Blake's Top Places
- *16 Croft Road, Hastings: blue plaque (often obscured)*
- *13 Sussex Square, Kemp Town, Brighton: formerly the Jex-Blake family home*
- *Rotherfield churchyard: headstone showing the names of Sophia Jex-Blake and Dr Margaret Todd*

SHEILA KAYE-SMITH
1887-1956

ST LEONARDS-ON-SEA

Sheila Kaye-Smith was a prolific Sussex author. She loved the countryside and, apart from an occasional foray into Kent, the eastern side of the county featured in almost all her work. When she died, the *New York Times* said that she was to Sussex what Thomas Hardy had been to Wessex; it was a good comparison, although (unlike Hardy) Sheila Kaye-Smith is rarely read today.

She was born at Battle Lodge, 9 Dane Road, in St Leonards. Her father was a local Battle doctor and both her parents were Anglicans. She attended St Leonards Ladies' College and spent summer holidays with her younger sister, Mona, at a local farm called Platnix. These later provided material for *The Children's Summer* (1932).

Sheila always knew she wanted to be a writer and began crafting stories while still a teenager. Her first full-length novel was *The Tramping Methodist*, which was published in 1908, when she was 21. Other novels followed and in 1916 she published *Sussex Gorse*, which told the story of an ambitious farmer, Reuben Backfield. Set in the areas she knew so well – Rye, Northiam and Peasemarsh – it was rich in vivid detail and dialect. It was a good read and it made Sheila Kaye-Smith famous; it was also, probably, the novel that Stella Gibbons parodied in *Cold Comfort Farm*.

Over the following decades, Sheila published more than 40 novels. Most featured rural Sussex and included issues such as farming, the changing situation of rural society and religion. She was very knowledgeable about farming matters and Sussex ways: in 1924 she wrote the preface to a reprint of John Coker Egerton's *Sussex Folk and Sussex Ways*. One of her best-known novels was *The End of the House of Alard* (1923). Based on a Peasemarsh family, it traced the decline of an aristocratic family after World War I; it also explored Roman Catholicism, which mirrored Sheila Kaye-Smith's changing religious beliefs.

In 1924 she married Theodore Penrose Fry, an Anglican clergyman whom she had met at the Anglo-Catholic Christ Church in St Leonards. They converted to Catholicism and moved to London, but returned to Sussex in 1929 and set up home near Northiam, living in a converted oast house called Little Doucegrove. They built a small Catholic church, St Teresa of Lisieux, on their land.

Sheila Kaye-Smith was not just a novelist. She published poems and short stories and wrote non-fiction, including a biography of John Galsworthy, a book on Anglo-Catholicism and a guidebook, *The Weald of Kent and Sussex*. Her novels were extremely popular during her lifetime; they captured Sussex absolutely and her admirers included Thomas Hardy, Noël Coward and her close friend Gladys Bronwyn Stern, with whom she collaborated on two books about Jane Austen.

In 1956 Sheila Kaye-Smith suffered a heart attack and died. She was buried in the churchyard of St Teresa of Lisieux. Her books fell out of fashion, although Virago reprinted two of her novels in the 1980s. In 1987 a Sheila Kaye-Smith Society was formed in St Leonards to revive interest in her work.

Sheila Kaye-Smith's Top Places
- 9 Dane Road, St Leonards: blue plaque
- Platnix Farm, Westfield: Sheila Kaye-Smith's childhood holiday location
- Little Doucegrove, near Northiam
- Church of St Teresa of Lisieux

Sheila Kaye-Smith's Top Works
- *Sussex Gorse*, 1916
- *Tamarisk Town*, 1919
- *The End of the House of Alard*, 1923
- *Joanna Godden Married and other Stories*, 1926
- *The Weald of Kent and Sussex*, 1953

DAME GRACE KIMMINS
1870-1954

CHAILEY

Grace Kimmins founded the first purpose-built school for physically disabled children in Britain. She called it her 'Public School
of Crippledom', a term that seems offensive today, but was
commonplace at the time. She was apparently seen as somewhat dicta-
torial, but she needed to be: through her untiring determination she
pioneered an innovatory approach to disability, based on her passionate
belief that even the most challenged could achieve self-esteem and independence through hard work, meaningful activity and encouragement.
Her memorial today is Chailey Heritage, which she founded in 1903.

Born in Lewes, Grace was the daughter of a cloth merchant, James
Hannam. Following her education she went to London, where, known
as Sister Grace, she joined a Wesleyan mission, working with poor and
underprivileged families in London's East End. She was particularly
concerned with the plight of impoverished children who had been physically disabled through tuberculosis, rickets, malnutrition or accidents.
Probably inspired by a popular sentimental Victorian novel, *The Story of a
Short Life* by Juliana Horatio Ewing, in 1894 she founded the first Guild of
Poor Things, a name she later changed to the Guild of Poor Brave Things.

Cleveland Hall in west London provided the first venue for Guild
meetings. Every week disabled people, adults and children, streamed
into the hall – on crutches, in wheelchairs or on foot, leading blind
friends by the hand – to be given tea, play activities and readings. For
Grace, the disabled were 'wounded soldiers, fighting the battle for an
independent life' and she devoted her life to them. She worked closely
with her lifelong friend, Alice Rennie, and received financial support
and encouragement from influential people, including the Duchess of
Bedford, Lady Emmeline Pethick-Lawrence and Mrs Millicent Fawcett,
whose husband had been blinded.

Grace's initial venture was successful and a year later she founded the Guild of Play, which, influenced by the ideas of art critic and thinker John Ruskin, stressed the importance of music, dance and play in children's lives. Weekly activities on offer increased to include lectures, craft classes, reading and singing – every meeting ended with a rousing and uplifting hymn. The Guild's motto was *Laetus soret mea* ('Happy in my lot'), a quote from Ewing's novel; and in its journal, *Child Life*, the Froebel Society described those who came to the Guild as 'a band of men, women and children of any creed or none, who are disabled for the battle of life, and at the same time are determined to fight a good fight'.

In 1898 Grace married child psychologist Charles William Kimmins. He was also an inspector of schools for the London County Council (LCC) and honorary treasurer of the Guild of Play. They had two sons and together continued the work Grace had started in providing educational and welfare for poor disabled children. Building on the initial success, a network of Guilds sprang up in London, Brighton, Hove and elsewhere, although many chose alternative names. Around this time too Grace wrote her only published novel, *Polly of Parker's Rents* (1899), describing children's lives in the slums.

By 1902 Grace had decided that the countryside would provide better therapeutic opportunities than London and determined to set up residential facilities for this purpose. She returned to Sussex, where she took over a derelict workhouse in Chailey. There was no gas, no electricity, the building was rat-infested and the nearest public telephone was at Plumpton. Nothing daunted, she had the building restored and brought down seven disabled London boys as the first residents. The boys helped with the renovation and the Chailey Heritage for Cripple Boys opened in 1903. With her husband's support and funds from philanthropic backers, she took over more derelict buildings, restored them and expanded the school. In 1908 a Heritage school for Cripple Girls was opened.

Grace Kimmins' work at Chailey attracted considerable attention. She believed profoundly that disabled children would find pride and self-sufficiency and the ability to mix in mainstream society through useful work. Under her leadership, Chailey became a major centre for poor disabled London school children. Cleverly she exploited her husband's links to the LCC, so that the children who came to Chailey were funded through the rates.

There had never been anything like the Chailey Heritage Craft Schools. They offered not just therapeutic and hospital facilities, but also a range of work and learning opportunities. The schools took in physically disabled children of all ages, from one-month-old babies to 16-year-olds. The sexes were strictly segregated: boys learned carpentry, leather craft, made their own boots and created furniture for the schools, producing tables, chairs and benches from local Sussex oak; girls were taught needlework, cooking and other housewifery skills. Games, gymnastics, music and movement were part of the programme.

During World War I more than 500 wounded soldiers were sent to Chailey for occupational training and rehabilitation, often learning to use prosthetic limbs. Grace Kimmins attended to their practical and emotional needs, and paired disabled soldiers with similarly disabled children, the boys often training the men. Soldiers were housed in the boys' quarters, and Chailey boys built new huts for themselves – known, patriotically, as Kitchener huts.

Grace also focused on fundraising, at which she was particularly skilled. She never lost an opportunity to promote Chailey and its work, circulating information and inviting the rich and well connected to visit at every possible opportunity and make donations. She attracted a number of formidable supporters, including Robert Baden-Powell and members of the royal family, who visited Chailey on at least two occasions.

As Chailey grew, Grace Kimmins kept control of every aspect of its running, earning her the nickname 'Commandant'. Under her direction, it offered an increasing range of facilities, taking on board new and innovatory developments. The eminent orthopaedic surgeon, Robert Jones, acted as a consultant, and Margaret Morris developed new forms of dance therapy for the disabled. In 1931 renowned child psychologist Cyril Burt described Chailey as 'a great demonstration laboratory where the best that can be done for the crippled child is… put into practice and tested'.

As money poured in – including £500 from a peer of the realm, £500 from the Duchess of Argyle and £2 from a one-armed pensioner – Chailey Heritage continued to expand, with more residential and hospital facilities, craft workshops and classrooms, gymnasiums, a laundry and a chapel. A devout Christian, Grace Kimmins encouraged different bishops and clerics to preach at Chailey, although, ever the practical woman, she operated a buzzer from the back of the chapel to warn any visiting cleric if she felt their sermon was overlong.

An energetic figure in a long dress and winged muslin cap, Grace ran Chailey on spartan but caring lines. She believed in the benefits of sunshine, sea air and bathing and insisted that children's cots and beds should be wheeled outside on every sunny day, winter or summer. Children often slept outside, as did she. In 1924 she also founded a Marine Hospital School at Tide Mills near Newhaven, where disabled boys received medical treatment and were also taught shipbuilding skills.

In 1927 Grace Kimmins' achievements were recognised when she was made a CBE, and then, in 1950, Dame of the British Empire. During World War II disabled soldiers were once more sent to Chailey, as were babies and children traumatised by the Blitz. In 1948 Chailey Heritage was incorporated into the newly formed National Health Service. Grace resigned, but continued to live at Chailey Heritage until her death.

In 2006, in an interview with the *Daily Telegraph*, her granddaughter, Mrs Hanbury, described Grace Kimmins as:

> a little lady with the heart of a lion, strong and passionate about her children. She had the ability to infect other people with her love of the place… my grandmother's great belief was that you should concentrate on your ability, not your disability. That was the unself-pitying legacy she left and it is as strong today as ever.

Dame Grace Kimmins' Top Place
⊙ *Chailey Heritage School, near Lewes: a special school for children with complex physical disabilities and associated learning problems*

Dame Grace Kimmins' Top Work
⊙ *Heritage Craft Schools and Hospital: 1903-1942*

THE LAWRENCE SISTERS
PENELOPE *1856-1932*   DOROTHY *1860-1933*
MILLICENT *1863-1925*

BRIGHTON

In 1946 *Time* magazine stated that 'the bouncy, bumpy Roedean Girl [was] a national byword, as British as roast beef and Yorkshire pudding…' – and even today the name Roedean conjures up a particular image of a particular type of public schoolgirl. The founders of Roedean (still one of the most distinguished private girls' schools in Britain) were three sisters: Penelope, Dorothy and Millicent Lawrence. The Roedean girls nicknamed them 'the Firm'.

The Lawrence sisters came from a large family, many of whom seemed to have an extraordinary propensity for teaching. Their father was Philip Lawrence, a solicitor and enthusiastic mineralogist, who married twice. His first wife was Charlotte Bailey, and Penelope was their only child. Charlotte died when Penelope was three months old, and in 1858 Philip married Margaret Davies, a gifted and energetic woman, who loved children. They lived in Wimbledon and had 13 children: seven boys and six girls.

During the 1860s the family spent periods of time abroad, in Germany and France. Penelope attended schools in Germany and studied for a Froebel teaching diploma; German governesses taught her sisters at home. From 1873 the family lived permanently in England, at Fearegg House, a huge mansion in Wimbledon that Philip had built.

With her father's encouragement, Penelope went to Newnham College, Cambridge, and in 1878 gained a Tripos in natural science, which was awarded by Trinity College, Dublin because Cambridge did not then award degrees to women. She stayed on at Newnham, working with women students in the physiology laboratory. From 1883 she taught part-time at Wimbledon High School. Dorothy studied at Bedford College, although poor health prevented her from achieving her degree, and Millicent did a teacher's training course paid for by Penelope.

In 1881 Philip injured himself while rock climbing and never worked again. Faced with the need to keep home and family together, Margaret, with Dorothy and Millicent's help, decided to set up a school for girls in Fearegg House. They took in paying boarders and day pupils and ran the school for four years. Combining home, school and the needs of an invalid was exhausting, so in 1885 Dorothy and Millicent suggested selling Fearegg House and starting their own school for girls somewhere else. They wrote to Penelope, then on holiday in Madeira, asking her to join them, which she did enthusiastically.

Casting about for a suitable place, the sisters fixed on Brighton. They rented a house in Lewes Crescent and opened their first school with ten pupils: 'six paying and four for show'. Two of their pupils were their younger sisters Christabel and Theresa: the latter went on to open a Roedean in South Africa. Pupil numbers grew, the sisters rented the house next door and then moved the school, now called Wimbledon House School, to larger premises in Sussex Square. Their aim was to 'give physical education and outdoor exercise their due place in every girl's life...to train each girl to independence and self-reliance [and]...to supply a sound and careful intellectual training'. They offered a full curriculum, including English, history, languages, music and domestic science, and also prepared girls for entrance to Newnham and Girton Colleges.

The sisters ran Wimbledon House School in a fairly relaxed fashion, incorporating clubs, societies, drama and plenty of outdoor sport into the school. Millicent was a first-class businesswoman and organiser, Penelope had drive and vision and Dorothy had the ability to bring out the best in her pupils. The school was successful, their parents joined them, and at one point all the Lawrence daughters were employed.

In 1895 the three sisters decided to set up an independent girls' school from scratch that would be the equal of any other independent school. With drive and determination they raised money, bought land from the Marquess of Abergavenny, Lord Lieutenant of Sussex, and employed the architect John W. Simpson to build them an imposing school in the grand manner. The foundation stone was laid in July 1897 and the school, consisting of four boarding houses, opened for business in October 1898.

From the start Roedean was run on the lines of a boys' public school: it was effectively the girls' equivalent of Eton. Games and physical activity were considered extremely important, as was academic achievement. The sisters dedicated themselves totally to Roedean, and each sister brought her own qualities to it. Penelope was an excellent and inspirational teacher; she organised the academic side of the school and, although not a sportswoman, promoted team games, believing they encouraged cooperation, discipline and obedience. She advocated swimming for health, and Roedean girls often watched amazed as her rather bulky form ploughed its way between the two piers in Brighton. Millicent taught maths and geography and managed the school's accounts. She became involved in local issues, was active in the Girl Guides and encouraged Roedean girls to do likewise, setting up a Girl Guide company at the school; she was also a suffragist. Dorothy was physically and emotionally frailer than her sisters. She devoted herself to the chapel, which was donated to the school in 1906, and developed the musical side of Roedean: girls always considered her to be most approachable and sympathetic member of 'the Firm'. Christabel Lawrence, founder of the All-England Women's Hockey Association, often oversaw games.

Roedean soon gained a reputation as an excellent girls' school with a fine academic and sports reputation. By 1906 it had 200 pupils and numbers continued to grow. The sisters retired in 1924, but not before giving the school the independent status that it has today. They also maintained contact with the school and pupils until they died. Today Roedean continues to flourish: it has just under 400 pupils, and fees per term range from just over £4,000 to more than £8,000.

The Lawrence Sisters' Top Places
⦿ Roedean School, just outside Brighton
⦿ Brighton bus, ID 851, and Metro Line 5: both display 'The Lawrence sisters' as part of their livery

DOROTHY (DOT) LEVITT

EARLY 1900s

BEXHILL, BRIGHTON

In 1905 Brighton onlookers were astonished when a raffish young woman established the women's world speed record, driving an 80-horsepower Napier in the annual speed trials. It was Dorothy Levitt, a secretary and society girl, and she caused a sensation, achieving a speed of 79 miles per hour (128 kph). The following year in Blackpool, driving a 90-horsepower six-cylinder Napier, she broke her own record and, driving at 91 miles per hour (146 kph), established another world speed record for women, although she 'had a near escape as front part of bonnet worked loose and, had I not pulled up in time, might have blown back and beheaded me'. In 1907 she was back in Sussex again, racing in Bexhill.

Surprisingly, little is known about Dorothy Levitt (her life dates, for instance, are not listed in any of the obvious sources), but she was the first-known British woman racing driver, the first to hold the ladies' world land-speed record and she pioneered the sport for women. Racing in a dust coat with matching hat and veil, she was a well-known figure on the racing scene in the early years of the 20th century.

Dorothy's early successes were in speed trials and long-distance races: Brooklands circuit did not open until 1907 and women were not allowed access until 1908: they could not compete against men. In April 1903 she became the first Englishwoman to take part in a public automobile competition. She 'did not win. Will do better next time.' She went on to race in France, achieved 994 points out of 1,000 on the non-stop London-Glasgow event and raced in the Southport speed trials. She also, in passing, won a race at Cowes, driving the motorboat Napier, and was presented to the King. Between 1903 and 1908 she raced several times a year in France, Germany and Scotland, as well as at Bexhill and Brighton, winning virtually every race.

In addition to being a superlative racing driver, Dot Levitt actively promoted motoring as an appropriate activity for women, challenging a widespread male prejudice. She wrote regular articles for the *London Daily Graphic*, and so many women wrote for advice that she expanded them into a book, *The Woman and The Car: A chatty little handbook for all women who motor or who want to motor*. Although written for women of a certain class – only the wealthy could afford motoring – it is a fascinating read and full of detail. She believed passionately that:

> *Motoring is a pastime for women: young, middle-aged, and – if there are any – old. There may be pleasure in being whirled around the country by your friends... or in a car driven by your chauffeur; but the real, the intense pleasure, the actual realisation of the pastime comes only when you drive your own car.*

She covered all aspects of the car, from its cost, upkeep and accessories, to mechanisms, oil, water and petrol checks, and provided a step-by-step guide to driving, which included advice on how to start a car:

> *In front of the car you will notice a handle. Push it inwards until you feel it fit into a notch, then pull it up sharply, releasing your hold of the handle the moment you feel you have pulled it over the resisting (compression) point... on no account press down the handle. If it is pressed down the possibility of a backfire is greater – and a broken arm may result...*

Other chapters gave advice on fixing problems, from water in the carburettor to faulty spark plugs. Dorothy Levitt obviously did all her own car maintenance, with one exception: 'It is possible for a woman to repair a tyre, but I am sure I am correct in saying that not one woman in a thousand would want to ruin her hands in this way.' She recommended finding a garage.

She also covered motoring manners – 'it lies with drivers to keep clear of pedestrians [but] dogs, chickens and other domestic animals... are not pedestrians and if one is driving at a regulation speed... one is not responsible for their untimely end' – and the 'all-important question of dress'. Photographs show her as a slight, attractive curly-haired woman sitting upright, with kid gloves firmly clasped on the steering wheel, or dressed in long skirt, hat and veil sorting out the mechanics of her car: dressing impeccably, but sensibly, was obviously important. She drove, on average, 400 miles (645 km) a week and listed essential items that she took with her: clean gloves, an extra handkerchief, a clean veil, powder puff, hair pins, chocolate and a small revolver. She always drove with an automatic Colt – essential for a single woman driving alone. Dorothy also advised carrying a mirror with a handle on it:

> to occasionally hold up to see what is behind you... you can, with the mirror, see in a flash what is in the rear, without losing your forward way and without releasing your right-hand grip of the steering wheel.

This wonderful woman invented the rear-view mirror some years before it was commercially produced in 1914.

Dorothy was apparently reluctant to talk about herself, but seems to have come from the West Country. Before she took up motoring she was a keen horsewoman and reminded women that cars – unlike horses – do not have brains. She was also an excellent shot. Her career took off when Australian businessman and racing driver Selwyn Francis Edge spotted her in her first competition drive and asked her to be his 'works driver', racing his Napier cars. She did so, but insisted on keeping amateur status.

She was very popular and lived in a bachelor flat in London's West End, with a housekeeper, a maid and a Pomeranian called Dodo. She threw and attended parties, mixed with an upper-class and sometimes bohemian set and travelled widely. It is not clear what happened to her after 1909.

Dorothy (Dot) Levitt's Top Place
- Bexhill Museum: material on early women motorists (but not on Dot Levitt)

Dorothy (Dot) Levitt's Top Work
- The Woman and The Car: A chatty little handbook for all women who motor or who want to motor (1909; reprinted 1970)

LYDIA LOPOKOVA
1 8 9 2 - 1 9 8 1

TILTON, NEAR FIRLE

Few more exotic women can ever have graced Sussex than Lydia Lopokova, ballet dancer and wife of John Maynard Keynes. She was born Lidiya Lopukhova (the spelling of her name was later anglicised) in St Petersburg, Russia, the daughter of a stage-struck usher at the Imperial Alexsandrinsky Theatre in St Petersburg and his wife Rosalia Constanza Karlovna Douglas. All their children were destined for a life in the ballet: one of their three sons, Fyodor, became chief choreographer of the Mariinsky Theatre and the second of their two daughters, Lidiya, found fame as principal ballerina of Serge Diaghilev's Ballets Russes – and later as the devoted wife of the economist John Maynard Keynes.

In 1901 Lydia was sent to the Imperial Ballet School, graduating to the Imperial Ballet in 1909. She joined the prestigious new Ballets Russes the following year for a tour of European cities and, although only 17, was already competent enough to partner Vaslav Nijinsky in *Carnaval and The Firebird* on occasions when the leading ballerina was unavailable. At the end of the season she, together with her sister and elder brother, set off to make her name as a dancer and actress in the United States, where she stayed for six years; she was never to dance in Russia again.

In 1916 the Ballets Russes toured America, and Lopokova rejoined Diaghilev's company as leading ballerina. She remained with the troupe after the end of the US tour, mainly because she had by then married Diaghilev's business manager, Randolfo Barocchi. Her return to Europe in 1918 secured her reputation as a great dancer, but also established her exuberant and rather irreverent personality. During a 1918 performance of *Les Sylphides* in London, she reached under her skirt, removed her frilly knickers and tossed them into the wings. Although this endeared her to many (and outraged a few), it indicated a less than serious attitude to her career.

In 1919 she suddenly left the company – and her husband – in London and disappeared for two years. Her disappearance shocked and mystified the ballet world. Just as mysteriously, however, she resurfaced in 1921 in Paris, once again dancing for Diaghilev in the Ballets Russes and re-establishing herself on the European stage, dancing the Lilac Fairy and Princess Aurora in *The Sleeping Princess*. The 1920s also saw her entry into European artistic society: she mixed with Stravinsky, T.S. Eliot and Picasso (who drew many pictures of her) and gained a reputation as a witty and entertaining companion. She also gained many famous admirers, among them John Maynard Keynes, whom she married in 1925 when her divorce from Barocchi became final. They moved to Tilton, near Firle, and divided their time between Cambridge, London and Sussex.

Initially, Keynes seemed an unlikely husband: he was a member of the notorious Bloomsbury set (*see p. 10*) and had had a homosexual affair with the artist Duncan Grant. His fellow 'Bloomsberries' thought he was homosexual and also saw Lydia as too lightweight and frivolous a partner for him, despite her wide circle of influential and intellectual friends. Virginia Woolf (*see p. 91*) commented that Keynes had fallen 'passionately and pathetically in love' and the Bloomsbury circle never really accepted Lydia. Their marriage inspired a slightly mocking couplet:

> *What a marriage of beauty and brains*
> *The fair Lopokova and John Maynard Keynes.*

However, the couple were absolutely devoted to each other and wrote daily letters whenever they were apart. Her infectious good humour was a perfect foil for his academic seriousness, prompting him to write during their courtship, 'How lucky we never bore one another. Can one go on being in love with someone who bores you?' For her part, Lydia greatly admired and supported her husband's economic theories and accompanied him on many of his trips abroad to promote his ideas. He, in turn, provided financial expertise to help promote the growing English ballet.

One of the reasons Keynes was so fascinated with Lydia was her wilful refusal to come to grips with the English language, preferring to amuse and confuse their friends with her idiosyncratic malapropisms, which he called 'Lydiaspeak' and she insisted were designed to 'enigmatise' him. She consistently referred to Lady Sibyl Colefax as Lady Colebox, and raised a few eyebrows when she described a visit to the bird-lover Lady Grey, saying, 'She has an ovary which she likes to show everyone.' Their letters were published in 1989 under the title *Lydia and Maynard* and are full of her almost poetic misuse of English. For example, 'I have a feeling of decay in me for a few days,' she wrote, going on, 'To-night my bed is willing to receive me, as I used my body in many yards of action.' Reassuring Keynes that her influence on him was beneficial, she said, 'In a way it is bad for you to listen to this chatter-boxing, but from a different angle it is good – because there is no-one's tongue like that in Cambridge.' But their correspondence touchingly shows their mutual affection, illustrated by her comment 'I am fond, pro-fond and re-fond of you', to which he replied, 'I kiss you and re-kiss you and pro-kiss you'.

Keynes continued his association with the Bloomsbury Group and they did visit Charleston together, but preferred to spend most of their time at Tilton, which was nearby. By now Lydia was only performing occasionally, choosing to devote most of her time to their home life. When Keynes became ill in 1937 she virtually ended her stage career: she spent her time helping him with his work and entertaining their friends. In 1942 Keynes was honoured with the title Baron Keynes of Tilton, and the irreverent, diminutive 'Loppy' became the respectable Lady Keynes.

Lydia's beloved husband died in 1946 and she virtually retired from public life, living mainly at Tilton. She died in Sussex at the Threeways Nursing Home, Seaford, aged 88.

Lydia Lopokova's Top Places

◉ *Tilton Farmhouse, Firle: Lopokova and Keynes's home*

◉ *National Gallery, London: The Awakening of the Muse, a mosaic, shows Lydia Lopokova as Terpischore, the muse of dancing*

LEE MILLER
1907-77

CHIDDINGLY

American fashion model, photographer and legendary beauty, Lee Miller started her life on a farm in Poughkeepsie, New York State and ended it on a farm in Sussex. In between she lived a restless, creative and often surreal life, in keeping with the Surrealism that characterises her finest work.

Her father Theodore Miller was a mechanical engineer and keen photographer, from whom she learned how to use a camera. When she was seven she was raped by a family friend and infected with venereal disease, which her mother treated with agonising douches of a mercury solution. The trauma must have fuelled her rebellious and sometimes desperate approach to life.

She was expelled from a series of schools in New York and then, aged 18, went to Paris to study theatre design and lighting. Gregarious and beautiful, Lee was immediately drawn to the bohemian life in Paris, mixing and forming friendships with, among others, Ernest Hemingway, Jean Cocteau and Gertrude Stein.

Her father brought her back to New York where, when she was 19, she encountered magazine publisher Condé Nast, who pulled her to safety just as she was about to meander in front of a car. This chance meeting launched her career as a fashion model. Lee's blonde hair, slim body and blue eyes suited the fashion of the time and by 1927 she was on the front cover of *Vogue* and soon working with all the leading American photographers. She modelled sportswear and svelte evening gowns, but in 1929 her sophisticated image was used to endorse Kotex sanitary towels, something that caused a scandal and brought her modelling career to an end.

Lee Miller was restless – she once commented that she 'looked like an angel but had a fiend inside' – and in 1929 returned to Paris to study photography with the Surrealist artist and photographer Man Ray. She stayed with him for three years, as his pupil, assistant and lover. They developed a photographic technique called solarisation and Miller progressed her own development as a professional photographer, adopting a witty and Surrealist style. She was part of the Surrealist movement in Paris and appeared as a statue in Jean Cocteau's film *Blood of a Poet* (1930). She set up a photographic studio, creating photographs such as *Exploding Hand* (now in London's Victoria and Albert Museum) and doing fashion assignments for leading designers such as Chanel. Around this time, too, she met and took another lover, an older wealthy Egyptian businessman called Aziz Aloui Bey.

The *ménage à trois* was complicated, not least because of Man Ray's obsessive jealousy, and Lee returned to New York where she opened a photographic studio, creating portraits such as *Floating Head* (1932), work for *Vogue*, *Harper's Bazaar* and *Vanity Fair*. She exhibited for the first time in 1932: Vanity Fair described her as 'one of the seven most distinguished living photographers'. In 1934 she suddenly married Bey and they went to Cairo, where she embarked on a hectic social round, gambling, drinking and learning Arabic, but also making long trips into the desert, where she photographed desert villages and extraordinary images of rock formations. She produced more than 2,000 photographs, one of the best known being *Portrait of Space*.

By 1937, leaving Bey in Egypt, she was back in Paris once more: within hours she met the British Surrealist painter Roland Penrose and they became lovers. She travelled with Penrose to the south of France, where Picasso painted four portraits of her, and also visited Egypt and the Balkans. In 1939 she separated from Bey and joined Penrose in London.

Lee Miller did her some of her most creative and spectacular photographic work during World War II. Although summoned back to the United States, she remained in London working for *Vogue*: initially she focused on war-torn London, capturing the impact of the Blitz and often juxtaposing images to create surreal masterpieces. In 1944 she was accredited to the US army and, teaming up with Time-Life photographer David Scherman (with whom she also had an affair), she went to Normandy straight after the D-Day landings and followed the US army advance across Europe. She photographed the American troops on Omaha Beach, and entered Paris with them on liberation day, becoming possibly the first woman combat photojournalist to enter the city. There she sought out and photographed old friends, including Picasso, Colette and Cocteau. She also photographed Fred Astaire dancing for the troops. Despite army regulations, she photographed combat on many occasions, witnessing the siege of St Malo and the Alsace campaign. She entered Buchenwald and Dachau concentration camps when they were liberated and photographed what she found there: the horrors haunted her, and her photographs, which were published in *Vogue*, shocked the British and American public. She and Scherman billeted in Hitler's house in Munich, where Scherman took a notorious photo of Miller in Hitler's bath, and she captured images of Hitler's burning mountain home at Berchtesgaden, just before the German surrender.

The end of the war left her discontented and unsettled. She travelled through Eastern Europe taking dramatic shots of the impact of war, photographing dying children in Vienna, peasants in Hungary and the execution of fascist leader László Bárdossy. She divorced Bey and in 1947 married Penrose, and they had a son, Anthony. Miller and Penrose bought Farley Farm near Chiddingly in Sussex, which became their home. It also became a meeting place for visiting artists, including Picasso, Man Ray, Henry Moore, Eileen Agar and Max Ernst, most of whom Miller photographed. She lost interest in journalism and took no professional assignments after 1954. She never talked about the war, but was increasingly hit by periods of depression, fuelled by alcohol and drugs. She died of cancer, aged 70. Her son later uncovered 40,000 negatives and 500 prints of her work, which he used as a basis for the Lee Miller Archive.

Lee Miller's Top Place

◉ *Farley Farm, Chiddingly: contains work by Lee Miller and Roland Penrose, plus work by Picasso, Man Ray, Max Ernst and others*

MARIANNE NORTH
1 8 3 0 - 9 0

HASTINGS

Marianne North epitomises a particular type of Victorian woman: she was a dutiful daughter and a determined individual who challenged convention. She came from a well-to-do and well-connected family. Her father, to whom she was devoted, was Frederick North, a magistrate and MP for Hastings, and her aunt was Countess Waldegrave (*see p. 83*). The family lived in Hastings Lodge, a large and imposing establishment, where they hosted balls and parties and where Marianne spent the first 40 years of her life.

It was a privileged upbringing. She was educated at home and learned singing and painting, accomplishments considered appropriate for young women of her class. She showed a skill for botanical painting and an early interest in plants, growing fungi in her room and visiting Kew Gardens to draw and paint rare specimens. She also travelled: in 1847 Frederick took the family on a three-year trip round Europe, during which Marianne took singing lessons, travelled along the Elbe, visited Prague and sketched and painted.

In 1855 her mother died, having first made Marianne promise that she would never leave her father – a promise that she fulfilled until his death. It was no hardship: for Marianne, her father was 'from first to last the one idol of my life'. The two lived and travelled together, visiting Egypt, Turkey and various other countries. Frederick died in 1869 and Marianne was deeply upset by his death, but would now realise a long-held dream 'of going to some tropical country to paint its peculiar vegetation in its natural abundant luxuriance'. She inherited her father's money and, as she chose to remain single – she had admirers, but thought marriage would be a 'terrible experience' – remained independent.

In 1871, aged 41, she left Hastings and travelled first to the United States, then to the Caribbean and Brazil, where, sitting in a hut in the jungle, she painted plants and flowers. She made a second solo journey to California, Borneo, Java and Ceylon (Sri Lanka), and in 1878-9 spent 15 months touring India.

Marianne North painted wherever she went, capturing in oils exotic plants and flowers native to every region she visited. Plant life fascinated her and she was prepared to go to any lengths – and any discomfort – to draw and paint inaccessible subjects. Although not formally trained, she produced glorious paintings, many of which were so exact in detail that they provided a valuable and lasting contribution to botanical knowledge. Some of the plants were unknown to European botanists and, as a result, were named after her.

She received support and encouragement from Joseph Hooker, director of Kew Gardens, who had been one of her father's friends, and regularly sent paintings back to Kew for safekeeping. Returning from India, she exhibited her work for the first time and donated her paintings to Kew, with the proviso that they should be housed in a special gallery – the Marianne North Gallery, which she funded.

In 1880, on the suggestion of Charles Darwin, Marianne set off again on an exhausting journey to Australia and New Zealand. She took a break from travelling in 1881-2 to decorate and supervise the hanging of her paintings in her gallery at Kew, then went to South Africa, returning to England in 1883. By now she was in failing health, but continued to travel and paint, journeying to Chile in 1884-5 to paint the monkey-puzzle tree; it was her final trip. In 1886 she retired to Gloucestershire, where she died, leaving her paintings and some highly readable journals.

Marianne North's Top Places

◉ Hastings Lodge, Hastings: later converted to a convent, now Marianne Park

◉ Marianne North Gallery, Royal Botanic Gardens, Kew: houses 832 of Marianne's paintings, depicting more than 900 plant species

Marianne North's Top Work

◉ Recollections of a happy life: being the autobiography of Marianne North, 1892: selections from her journals, edited by her sister, Catherine North Symonds

LADY JOAN PELHAM
d. 1439

PEVENSEY

L ady Joan Pelham is remembered in Sussex for two reasons: she successfully held Pevensey Castle against an armed siege, and she may well have been the first woman to write a letter in English. Whether this is so is still debated, but the letter is fascinating for its lack of panic.

There are very few details about Lady Pelham, and what exists is confused; her life dates and parentage are uncertain. However, it is known that she married Sir John Pelham, who was constable of Pevensey Castle. Sir John was a supporter of Henry Bolingbroke, Duke of Lancaster and son of John of Gaunt. In 1399 Henry Bolingbroke led an uprising against Richard II and claimed the English throne for himself. He landed at Pevensey from exile and set off for Yorkshire, taking Lord Pelham with him.

Lady Pelham was left behind at Pevensey Castle; this was not unusual for noble women in the medieval period, many of whom ran large estates and households while their husbands were away fighting. During his absence, however, the castle was attacked and besieged by Richard II's forces. With the assistance of only a small garrison, Lady Pelham courageously withstood the siege and rebuffed the King's army. She had no idea where her husband was and no way of contacting him to ask for help. At some point a letter arrived from Lord Pelham informing her that he was at Pontefract. She could now contact him, which she did in the letter quoted below. The original text was written in an older form of English, but has subsequently been translated into a more modern version to make it easier for modern readers to understand.

The letter is wonderful and, given Lady Pelham's circumstances, extraordinarily restrained. She begins with a loving greeting to her husband, and thanks for his safety, and not until she has done this does she explain that she is besieged and would welcome some help. Lady Pelham must have been not only well schooled in reading, writing and courtly manners, but also a rather courageous woman.

> My dear Lord – I recommend me to your high Lordship, with heart and body
> and all my poor might. And with all this I thank you as my dear Lord, dearest
> and best beloved of all earthly Lords, with all this that I said before of [for] your
> comfortable letter that you sent me from Pontefract, that came to me on Mary
> Magdalen's day: for by my trooth I was never so glad as when I heard by your
> letter that ye were strong enough, with the grace of God for to keep you from the
> malice of your enemies… And my dear Lord, if it like you to know my fare, I am
> here laid by in manner of a siege with the country of Sussex, Surrey and a great
> parcel of Kent so that I may not [go] out nor no victuals get me, but with much
> hard. Wherefore, my dear, if it like you by the advice of your wise counsel for to
> set remedy of the salvation of your Castle, and withstand the malice of the Shires
> aforesaid… Farewell, my dear Lord. The Holy Trinity keep you from your
> enemies… Written at Pevensey, in the Castle, on St Jacob's day last past.

Having sent her letter, Lady Pelham continued to defend Pevensey Castle, pacing the parapets every day until reinforcements arrived and routed the King's forces. When Bolingbroke became Henry IV, he rewarded Lord and Lady Pelham with new titles and land.

As a postscript, it is said that Lady Pelham's ghost haunts Pevensey Castle and there are recorded sightings. However, some say the ghost is that of Queen Joanna of Navarre, who was accused of witchcraft and imprisoned at Pevensey Castle in the early 1400s.

Lady Joan Pelham's Top Place
> *Pevensey Castle, Pevensey: site of the siege, now run by English Heritage*

CLARE SHERIDAN
1885-1970

BREDE PLACE

culptor, writer, journalist, traveller and possibly spy, Clare Sheridan was an extraordinary woman. She was born Clare Consuelo Frewen in London, the only daughter of Moreton Frewen, whose family has owned Brede Place in Sussex since 1616, and his American wife, Clara Jerome, daughter of an American millionaire. The family was extremely wealthy and well connected, owning land not only in Sussex, but also in Ireland and a town house in London. Clare's cousin was Winston Churchill.

Clare was educated at home in England and Ireland and attended schools in Paris and Germany. At the appropriate age she entered fashionable society, but wanted more from life than parties. She showed an early interest in writing and, with support from family friends such as Henry James and Rudyard Kipling, attempted some early novels.

In 1910 she married Wilfred Sheridan, descendant of the dramatist Richard Brinsley Sheridan, and they had three children. Her second daughter Elizabeth died of meningitis when she was only a few months old. Grief-stricken, Clare modelled a weeping angel for her daughter's grave and it is said that this is when she discovered her talent for sculpting. Not much more than a year later her husband died too, at the Battle of Loos, leaving Clare a widow with children to support. She moved to London, where she became a professional and highly regarded portrait sculptor. Her subjects included H.G. Wells, Asquith, Marconi, Gandhi and Churchill, whom she sculpted while he was painting a portrait of her. The National Portrait Gallery exhibited her work.

As a communist, Clare Sheridan was sympathetic to the revolutionary events taking place in Russia. In 1920 the first Soviet trade delegation arrived in London and invited her to the Soviet Union to sculpt leading revolutionaries. To the horror of her anti-Bolshevik cousin, she accepted and, although refused a visa, sailed first to Stockholm and then travelled through Estonia to Moscow. While there she sculpted bronze busts of Lenin, Zinoviev, Kamenev, Dzherzhinski and Trotsky. She later wrote:

> I asked him [Trotsky] to take off his pince-nez, as they hampered me. He hates doing this, he says he feels... absolutely lost without them. It seemed akin to physical pain taking them off... it is a pity as they rather spoil an otherwise classical head.

She spent a great deal of time with Trotsky, whom she admired enormously, and there were rumours of an affair; his secretary later said there had been 'an element of flirtation'. Clare enjoyed her time in the Soviet Union, saying, 'this place has spoilt one for brains, everyone is so brilliant'. She wrote lively accounts of her trip, published in 1921 as *Russian Portraits in Britain* and as *Mayfair to Moscow* in the United States.

She returned to England, to be given the cold shoulder not only by her cousin, but also by London society in general. She left for the United States and landed a job as European correspondent and roving reporter for the *New York World*. She also met and became friendly with Charlie Chaplin. Once again the rumour mill went into overdrive: she was surprised to read in the newspapers that they were engaged – which they were not.

The next few years were action-packed as she travelled through Europe, America and Mexico, having adventures and making her name as a journalist and war correspondent. She obtained interviews from Irish revolutionary leader Michael Collins and his opponent Rory O'Connor, covered the Greek-Turkish War, produced a moving account of the evacuation of Smyrna and interviewed the Turkish president, Atatürk, and Spanish politician Primo de Rivera, among others. Mussolini invited her to Italy for an interview, but would not allow it to be printed.

In 1923 Clare returned to the Soviet Union to write articles for the *World*, but this time she was disillusioned, which made her unpopular with the Soviet authorities. Even so she obtained a visa to travel through southern Russia, which she did on a motorbike, sitting in the sidecar while her brother drove. She went by ship to Constantinople (Istanbul) and lived for a while with her children on the Bosphorus. In 1925 she and her children moved to Algeria: she built a house on the edge of the Sahara desert, where they lived for some years.

Clare now began switching from writing back to sculpture. In 1937 her son Dick died of appendicitis, aged 21. She put her grief into carving a Madonna from a Sussex oak tree at her Brede Place home. Wanting to develop her woodcarving skills, she spent time with Native Americans on a Canadian reservation. She also exhibited Native American carvings in London, describing her experiences in *Redskin Interlude* (1938).

After World War II Clare Sheridan became a Roman Catholic and moved to Ireland, continuing her carvings, sculptures and writing. She died on May 31st 1970 and is buried at Brede Place. *The Times* called her 'a woman of varied talents': one of her biographers described her as:

> *beautiful, fearsome, an English aristocrat, a communist spy, a loose woman, a doting mother, an impossible parent, an inspired artist, a respected professional journalist, a middling novelist… imperious… restless, reckless, and liable to pop up anytime, anywhere and [with] anyone – often trailing ominous whiffs of scandal behind her.*

Whether she actually was a spy is debated. In 2002 *The Independent* published an article ('Churchill's Bolshevik cousin was Soviet informer') claiming that she passed on conversations with Churchill and other politicians to William Ewer, a key figure in Soviet intelligence. The *Glasgow Herald* came up with an intriguing counter-theory, namely that Churchill had hoped to use her to gain information about the Bolsheviks, but that the episode was 'still shrouded in some degree of mystery'.

Clare Sheridan's Top Places

- Belmont House, Belmont Road, Hastings: blue plaque
- Brede Place: contains busts by Clare Sheridan of Churchill, Gandhi, Lenin and Trotsky
- Brede parish church: her statue of the Madonna and Child, carved out of local oak
- All Saints church, West Dean: bust of Oswald Birley

Clare Sheridan's Top Works

- Turkish Kaleidoscope, 1926
- Arab Interlude, 1936
- To the Four Winds, 1957

CHARLOTTE SMITH
1749 - 1806

BIGNOR PARK

Charlotte Smith was a leading 18th-century writer who, like her contemporary Mary Wollstonecraft, had a troubled and difficult life. She was born in London, the daughter of Nicholas Turner, a profligate landowner whose property included Bignor Park on the River Arun in Sussex. When she was about three her mother died in childbirth. Charlotte was sent to her aunt and went to school in Chichester and London. She loved reading and, unknown to her aunt, who was not a literary person, used her pocket money to subscribe to a circulating library, spending hours 'running through all the trash it contained'.

Charlotte's childhood was spent between London, Surrey and Bignor Park. She loved Sussex, particularly the South Downs, and images of the landscape recur throughout her writing. Her childhood ended abruptly when her father remarried. His new wife and Charlotte did not get on and in 1765, when she was 15, she was married off to Benjamin Smith, son of a merchant whose wealth came from a sugar plantation in the Caribbean. Charlotte said her father sold her into marriage like a 'legal prostitute'.

The couple moved to Cheapside, where Charlotte's father-in-law ran his business – it was a stark contrast to Sussex, and her new family were not welcoming. Her first child was born in 1766, but died days after the birth of her second: in all she had 12 children, but only six survived her.

The marriage was not a good one. Benjamin Smith was a reckless gambler, a drunk and could be violent. However, Charlotte's father-in-law, Richard Smith, recognised her qualities: he appreciated her literary ambitions and she helped him with his business affairs. When he died in

1776 he left most of his property to his grandchildren, but the will was disputed and a Chancery suit began that rumbled on for years: Dickens possibly based *Bleak House* on it.

Benjamin Smith spent wildly in anticipation of the legacy and in 1783 was sent to debtors' prison. Charlotte accompanied him for a while and, knowing that she needed to earn money, wrote her first book. With help from the poet William Hayley, a Sussex neighbour who assisted other writers including William Blake, her poems were published, albeit at her own expense. *Elegiac Sonnets, and Other Essays* by Charlotte Smith of Bignor Park, Sussex appeared in 1784. Her poems such as 'Sonnet V: To the South Downs' were in the Romantic style, sombre, often melancholic and full of Sussex references:

> And you, Aruna, in the vale below,
>> As to the sea your limpid waves you bear,
> Can you one kind Lethean cup bestow
>> To drink a long oblivion to my care?
> Ah no! When all, e'en hope's last ray, is gone,
>> There's no oblivion but in death alone!

Elegiac Sonnets was an immediate success; a second edition was published within a year and by 1800 the book was in its ninth edition, establishing Smith as a serious literary figure. Southey praised her work, and her sonnets influenced Coleridge and Wordsworth, who later commented that she was 'a lady to whom English verse is under greater obligations than are likely to be either acknowledged or remembered'.

When Benjamin came out of prison, the family went to France to escape his debtors, but Charlotte was increasingly scared of her husband, whose temper was now 'so capricious and often so cruel'. They returned to England in 1785 and lived in Midhurst, but in 1787 she finally left him although he continued to demand money from her.

Settling near Chichester, she decided to support her children with her writing until the legacy was settled. In the late 1780s she turned to novels, although she always considered herself a poet. Between 1788 and 1798 she wrote 11 novels. Loosely using the popular Romantic formula of the day, she wove her own bitter experiences and angers into her writing. In her first novel, *Emmeline* (1788), she satirised her husband; in others she attacked greedy merchants who made their wealth on the back of slavery; vilified lawyers and trustees who kept their children's legacies from them; and wrote of women's oppression at the hands of men.

She wrote during revolutionary times and in her novel *Desmond* (1792), which described a man's desire for a married woman – quite shocking at the time – expressed her sympathies for the French Revolution, making her one of the-so called 'Jacobin' writers and winning admiration from radicals such as Tom Paine, William Godwin and Mary Wollstonecraft. As conditions intensified in France and war broke out, her general reading public became less sympathetic and being, as she described, 'a slave of the Booksellers', she shifted the setting of one of her most successful novels, *The Old Manor House* (1793), to the American Revolution.

Charlotte Smith's books were popular, but her political views and her tendency to write about her personal tragedies irritated some. Mary Wollstonecraft publicly supported her, but her reading public began to desert her and her popularity and earnings waned. During her final years, increasingly disabled with what was probably rheumatoid arthritis, she tried to improve her earnings by writing four books for children, a history of England and a book on natural history. She also wrote two more works of verse: *The Emigrants* (1793) and *Beachy Head* (1807). She died in Tilford, near Farnham in 1806.

Charlotte Smith's Top Places
- *Bignor Park: the Turner family home*
- *The South Downs and the River Arun: childhood settings, and recurrent images in Charlotte Smith's writing*

Charlotte Smith's Top Works
- *Elegiac Sonnets, and Other Essays by Charlotte Smith, 1784*
- *Emmeline, or the Orphan of the Castle, 1788*
- *Desmond, 1792*
- *The Old Manor House, 1793*
- *The Young Philosopher, 1798*
- *Beachy Head, 1807*

VESTA TILLEY
1 8 6 4 - 1 9 5 2

BRIGHTON

Vesta Tilley was a celebrated male impersonator and one of the most successful music-hall artists: during the 1890s she was the highest-earning woman in Britain. She brilliantly combined a clear, crystal voice with male outfits to produce a unique act that was very popular, particularly among women, who greatly enjoyed her mocking approach to the vagaries of male behaviour. Her life touched Brighton on many occasions: she frequently graced the boards at the Brighton Hippodrome, honeymooned in the town and in 1947, when she was 83, bought a holiday flat in Hove.

The story of Vesta Tilley is almost stereotypical: from working-class origins in Worcester through to high society in London and Monte Carlo. She claimed, however, that she never forgot her origins. And, no matter how outrageous her act might have appeared, she was somewhat conservative and was never touched by scandal.

She was born Matilda Alice Powers, the second of 13 children, and her father, a china glazer turned comic and theatrical manager, was her first manager. She first appeared on stage, singing and dancing, when she was either three or four. Under her father's direction, she began performing regularly and was usually billed as 'The Great Little Tilley', 'Tilley' being her abbreviation of Matilda. When she was about six she appeared on stage in boy's clothes as 'Pocket Sims Reeves' impersonating a famous adult music-hall performer of the day called Sims Reeves. The act was an immediate hit. From then on, dressing in male clothes became her trademark and she went on to develop a series of brilliantly observed male characters, from soldiers and sailors to the smart or foppish man-about-town. She also adopted the stage name by which she is known: Vesta, after Swan Vesta matches – she was sometimes billed as the 'bright spark' – and Tilley (as before).

In 1888 her father died, and in 1890 Vesta Tilley married Walter de Frece, the son of a Jewish theatre owner. Their marriage was happy and Walter, who founded the chain of Hippodrome theatres and music halls, became her manager, wrote some of her songs and, during the 1890s, assisted her to become a major and much-loved performer. Her songs and characters became household names: dressed in exquisite evening clothes, she thrilled audiences, singing 'Burlington Bertie' who rose 'at 10.30' in a delightful soprano. Working-class audiences in particular enjoyed the way she poked fun at the foppish male.

Her act was not just a matter of donning male clothes: her attention to detail was meticulous, according to whichever character she was portraying. Vesta Tilley had a range of beautifully made costumes, from frock coats and evening tails through to morning suits, sporting and military outfits. She wore men's underwear – women were still corseted at the time, which would have spoilt the illusion – and, when dressed as a soldier, even carried a full military kitbag for authenticity. She was also committed to making her act suitable for the whole family. Music hall had a somewhat smutty reputation, but, to her pride, her performances were always 'clean': she avoided double entendre and vulgarity.

Vesta Tilley became a household name. She toured Britain and Australia and also took her act to the United States, where she performed on the vaudeville circuit, being paid $600 a week by one theatre. It was a break-through: very few music-hall artists gained success outside Britain and she was a stupendous success. She also, in 1898, made some of the first gramophone recordings in Britain.

In 1912 she appeared at the first ever Royal Command Performance, to perform before Queen Mary and King George VI. Sadly, this occasion was not a personal triumph; apparently, when she appeared on stage dressed in men's clothes, the Queen and her ladies-in-waiting all covered their faces with their programmes rather than see a woman's legs. Interestingly, though, in 1924, as Lady de Frece, she was presented at court.

When World War I began, Vesta Tilley and her husband threw their efforts into performing for the troops and recruiting men for war. Dressed as a British 'Tommy', she performed patriotic numbers, including 'The Army of Today's Alright', 'Jolly Good Luck to the Girl who Loves a Soldier' and 'Your King and Country Want You', better known as 'We don't want to lose you but we think you ought to go'.

Vesta Tilley would then urge men to enlist, which they did to such an extent that she became known as 'England's Greatest Recruiting Sergeant' – something that, as the dreadful casualties rose, lost her some working-class support.

In 1919 Walter was knighted in recognition of his wartime services and Vesta Tilley became Lady de Frece. Walter decided he would run for Parliament as a Conservative MP, and in 1924 he was elected MP for Blackpool. It was no longer appropriate for Lady de Frece to be a music-hall star. Following a sell-out tour in 1919-20 she retired from the stage. Her final performance was to a packed house in London's Coliseum. When she finished, the audience gave her a 40-minute standing ovation and Ellen Terry presented her with a 'People's Testimonial' book bearing two million signatures – evidence, according to the *Daily Telegraph*, of 'warm admiration of an artistic genius'.

Following Walter's retirement in 1932 the couple moved to Monte Carlo. It was here that Vesta Tilley wrote her autobiography and, after Walter's death in 1935, returned to England, where she died on September 16th 1952, aged 88.

Vesta Tilley's Top Places
- *Bingo Hall, Middle Street, Brighton: formerly the Brighton Hippodrome*
- *8 St Aubyns Mansions, Kings Esplanade, Hove: formerly Vesta Tilley's apartment*

Vesta Tilley's Top Works
- *Recollections of Vesta Tilley, 1934*
- *The album Tipping the Velvet, released June 1st 2006, includes two of Vesta Tilley's recordings: 'Burlington Bertie from Bow' and 'Jolly Good Luck to the Girl who Loves a Soldier'*

SARAH, COUNTESS WALDEGRAVE
1787-1873

HASTINGS

Sarah, Countess Waldegrave was absolutely the product of her time and status. A redoubtable woman, she came from a solidly Anglican background and remained a devout Christian throughout her life. Her religion, combined with considerable wealth, made her the leading philanthropist in Victorian Hastings.

Sarah was born in Hastings Old Town Rectory, the younger daughter of the Reverend William Whitear, rector of All Saints and St Clements. She was probably taught at home and no doubt Bible studies played a part in her upbringing. When she was 30 she married Edward Milward, the son of an extremely wealthy and prominent local family. Both her husband and her father-in-law (also Edward Milward) were leading lights in the locality and had been Hastings mayors. By association Mrs Milward too involved herself in the community.

Edward Milward died in the 1830s, leaving Sarah an extremely wealthy woman, with a lifetime interest in the Milward estates. Later she married again, this time to William, 8th Earl Waldegrave, becoming as a result a countess and member of the aristocracy. Together with William Drew Shadwell, she was the largest landowner in the area and continued her first husband's tradition of public spiritedness.

Hastings was at this time going through major social and economic changes: James Burton started developing fashionable St Leonards during the 1820s and 1830s, a task continued by his son, Decimus Burton; the railway reached Hastings in 1846, and the town was becoming a popular seaside and holiday destination. The local population was growing rapidly, but poverty was extreme, particularly in the Old Town.

First as Mrs Milward and subsequently as Countess Waldegrave, Sarah used her wealth to provide Hastings with spiritual and practical assistance. She founded seven churches, including St Clements church, Halton, in 1838 (it was demolished in the 1970s) and St Andrew's church, Fairlight, in 1845. Her individual donations ranged from £500 to £1,000, a substantial sum for the time; she also gave land, stone and in some cases funded the furnishings. By all accounts she was not slow to interfere in any public project. She examined building plans scrupulously, made whatever comments and changes she wanted, and no project was permitted to proceed without her total approval. She laid the foundation stone for each church and took every opportunity to make a speech condemning any 'papacy'.

Countess Waldegrave believed it was her public duty to help the poor. She funded one of the first Sunday Schools in Britain and helped to set up schools for poor boys and girls in the Old Town. The Hastings Parochial School Society had been founded in 1835 with a remit to focus on educating the poor, and Sarah provided a house (formerly owned by the Milwards) to be used as a school. On her suggestion, it was funded partly by voluntary subscriptions and partly by small amounts from the pupils. As always, her donations came with conditions attached: she was adamant that there should be separate entrances for boys and girls. If boys were ever seen entering the school through the girls' entrance, which was in Tackleway, she would instantly take back the house. Similarly she allowed public access to her land at Ecclesbourne Glen and Lover's Seat, but strictly forbade people from taking alcohol with them.

She also gave money for wash houses and public baths, to be built in the Old Town, something she described as her 'gift to the poor'. It was a popular donation: the area of All Saints was particularly impoverished and washing facilities in the poor dwellings were extremely limited. The wash houses had separate rooms for washing, drying and ironing and enabled women of the Old Town to supplement the family income by taking in laundry. They opened in 1865 with a tea party for '40 poor laundresses' and Countess Waldegrave publicly washed one of her handkerchiefs.

Sarah's philanthropic interests were extensive. She involved herself in the Hastings Literary and Scientific Association, a society formed to set up circulating libraries, a museum and lectures, and in 1839 she donated a statue of Hygea, goddess of health, which she felt was 'particularly suited to Hastings', plus three pottery vases. Responding to the prevailing fear that another Napoleon might arrive at any time, she also funded the local Rifle Corps, donating £250 for clothing and allowing a drill ground and rifle range on her estates. Her final gift to the town was a donation of £800 to be used for a Fisherman's Institute in the Old Town. Always combining morality with practical welfare, she said that while she wanted this to be 'a resort in business hours', she also hoped it would provide 'a decided religious and moral influence for good'. The Institute, which was housed in Hughenden Hall, opened in 1882 and flourishes to this day, although the emphasis is very much on socialising rather than morality.

From all accounts Sarah, Countess Waldegrave was a serious and highly autocratic woman, described by Manwaring Baines as 'a masterful old lady'. She was never slow to impose her wishes and conditions on her gifts, and saw herself as leading the community – so much so on the occasion of the wedding of the sister of Marianne North (see p. 70) that she was only just prevented from giving the bride away. However, she did make the first speech. Although she imposed strict conditions on her donations, she made them nevertheless and the town greatly appreciated her philanthropy. In 1861, 12 years before she died, the people of Hastings erected a drinking fountain in Robertson Street in her honour. The inscription read:

In recognition of the constant support by her to the religious and benevolent institutions of the Borough and the neighbourhood. The money for this fountain was collected by the inhabitants of Hastings and St Leonards including the pence of children and young persons educated in the National Schools.

Sarah, Countess Waldegrave' Top Places
- *Roberston Street, Hastings: drinking fountain, next to Holy Trinity church*
- *All Saints' Street, Old Town, Hastings: the Fisherman's Institute*
- *Hastings Country Park: Ecclesbourne Glen and Lover's Seat*
- *Fairlight: St Andrew's church*
- *Old Hastings House (formerly The Mansion): portrait at Countess Waldegrave's home*
- *Waldegrave Street, Hastings*

MARY WHEATLAND
1835-1924

BOGNOR

Bognor may be best known for King George V's alleged last words 'bugger Bognor', but perhaps it should be better known for Mary Wheatland, 'Bognor's mermaid', who saved at least 30 souls from drowning.

Mary Wheatland was Sussex through and through. She came from Aldingbourne, a village east of Chichester, and when she was 14 arrived in Bognor, where she began working for a Mrs Mills, who owned and operated bathing machines. Bognor was by now a fairly flourishing resort, although not yet of Regis status. Not all would-be bathers were good swimmers, which is where Mary's skills came in; she was an excellent and powerful swimmer. She learnt to dive from the pier and often spent an hour or so swimming for her own amusement, despite being encumbered by the heavy costumes of the period. She became notorious for her habit of diving underwater and standing on her head, waving her legs in the air, something she continued until the ripe old age of 71.

During Mary's initial summer in Bognor she made her first successful rescue, a small Frenchwoman, whose cries could be heard on the beach as she floated helplessly towards the horizon. Other rescues followed, including the wife of a London brewer, whom Mary rescued from the water just as her 'soul was drifting into eternity and her body across the Channel'. No matter how rough the sea, Mary would dive in, swim out to the victim and drag them back safely to shore. Among the many people who owed their lives to her were six giddy young women who got into dreadful difficulties: according to an observer, they were 'all drowning in a bunch' until Mary, at considerable risk to her own life, swam around behind them and shepherded them to safety.

In 1857 Mary married George Wheatland and they moved to South Bersted on the outskirts of Bognor. They had a large family and Mary combined motherhood with work on the beach. The local vicar recorded her life-saving achievements in the parish magazine. Eventually she went into business for herself, operating and hiring out her own bathing machines and giving swimming lessons to visitors and girls from local private schools, possibly becoming the first woman to teach swimming. Her husband died in 1881, leaving her the sole breadwinner.

By all accounts Mary Wheatland was a kind, brave and modest woman. To show their gratitude, many of the people she rescued gave her money, but she made light of her achievements. Speaking of the six young women, she commented, 'Pray don't say anything about it, for they were very good to me; they gave me £2 towards back rent, and sent me a bit of beef at Christmas.' She thought saving lives was as much her work as rinsing a bathing dress.

Mary became a well-known and popular figure. In 1879 *The London Illustrated News* ran an article on her. The National Humane Society awarded her two certificates and a gold and silver medal, and Viscount FitzAlan presented her with a so-called Golden Penny for her courageous rescue of the six young women. The photographer, William Pankhurst Marsh, immortalised her in photographs, showing her resplendent with her medals. The photos were turned into postcards with an accompanying text that read:

> *a little old woman stands on the parade of Bognor looking out to sea. She is clad in a blue serge costume on the bodice of which two lifesaving medals are pinned. A battered sailor hat, bearing her name in gold letters, is tied under her chin with black ribbons. The weather beaten face is crumpled up into a network of smiles.*

In 1909 Mary Wheatland retired. She died on April 1st 1924, aged 89, at her home in Ivy Lane, South Bersted. Bognor mourned her death and local fishermen carried her coffin.

Mary Wheatland's Top Places

◉ *Bognor Regis Museum, High Street, Bognor: Mary Wheatland display*
◉ *St Mary Magdalene parish church, Bognor: burial place of Mary Wheatland; also a memorial bench*

VIOLET GORDON WOODHOUSE
1871-1948

FOLKINGTON

In the musical world Violet Gordon Woodhouse is remembered as a fine musician who helped to pioneer the English revival in early musical instruments, notably the clavichord and harpsichord. But she is perhaps equally well known for her colourful and unconventional personal life.

She was born Kate Eglinton Gordon Gwynne in Harley Street, London, the second daughter and fourth child of Mary (May) Earle and James Eglinton Gwynne. An inventor and engineer with an unpredictable temper, Gwynne was a wealthy landowner and in 1876 bought two country estates in East Sussex: Folkington and Wooton.

Violet spent much of her early life in Folkington. Her mother was a talented singer, who encouraged music in the family, and Violet learnt to play the piano and by the age of seven was showing a remarkable musical talent. Keen to foster this talent, her mother asked a celebrated concert pianist to teach Violet, which at first he refused to do, saying that he only accepted the most gifted. On hearing her play, he changed his mind, and by the age of 16 she was one of Oscar Beringer's most promising pupils.

Through her mother's musical contacts in London, Violet was introduced to a number of professional musicians and now decided on a career as a professional musician herself, something her father strenuously opposed. Marriage would mean escaping his authoritarian control and in 1893 Violet became engaged to Lord Gage, a Sussex landowner. On her mother describing the facts of life to her, Violet promptly broke off the engagement – whatever she was told obviously did not appeal. Two years later, however, she married Gordon Woodhouse. Violet made it quite clear that there were to be no children and certainly no sex, and Woodhouse, who was always devoted to Violet, accepted the terms. It is possible that, as a result of an unspecified hunting accident, he may not have been too disappointed.

By the mid-1890s Violet was increasingly attracted to early English music, which at that point had fallen out of favour and, if played at all, was played on the piano. She met Arnold Dolmetsch and, hearing his lecture recitals, was drawn to the harpsichord and clavichord. She took lessons with Dolmetsch and a programme survives of a Dolmetsch/Woodhouse concert in Violet's drawing room in December 1899, when she played the harpsichord. In 1894 she met the great Spanish cellist Augustín Rubio, who was another important mentor, advising her in particular on phrasing. He did not really mind which keyboard instrument she played, but after 1905 she ceased to play the piano, concentrating exclusively on harpsichord and clavichord. Through Rubio she developed a love of playing with cellists: she later performed with Joseph Holbrooke and Boris Hambourg in 1905, with Pablo Casals in 1924 and with Antoni Sala in 1930 at the Wigmore Hall, London.

Violet was a spectacular-looking woman – she apparently inherited her rather dark good looks from her grandmother, said to be descended from an Indonesian rani or queen; she also had an intelligent and vivacious personality. In 1899 her personal life took an unorthodox turn when the Honourable William Barrington fell passionately in love with her, something he confessed to her husband. She reciprocated his feelings and he moved into their home. It is possible that their relationship was sexual, but Gordon, who would do anything for Violet's happiness, seems not to have minded.

As if a *ménage à trois* was not enough, two other men now entered the household: the Honourable Denis Tollemache, a soldier and musician, and witty barrister Maxwell Labouchère. The fact that Violet was now living in a *ménage à cinq*, with four 'husbands', caused many raised eyebrows, but the five lived contentedly together. Labouchère died in World War I and Tollemache in World War II; Barrington and Woodhouse continued living together after Violet died.

Women, too, were strongly attracted to Violet. Novelist Radclyffe Hall was devoted to her, and composer Dame Ethel Smyth adored her, saying that 'harpsichord playing such as Violet's… is but one manifestation of a natural, effortless kinship with beauty in every form'.

Although Violet was mainly performing in private from her home, she was also achieving success and fame through public performances. After World War I, financial necessity meant that Violet had to turn professional and she played in various towns throughout England, including Eastbourne. Her recitals were well received. In 1920 she became the first to record harpsichord music, and in 1924 made the first-ever solo harpsichord broadcast.

In the late 1920s a strange quirk of fate meant that she was able to bring her public performances to an end. Her husband's spinster sisters were murdered by their butler and, since they had not left legally binding wills, Woodhouse inherited their fortune and bought Nether Lypiatt Manor, a beautiful 17th-century house in Gloucester. Violet now returned to playing in the drawing room of her own house, creating a renowned musical salon and performing to private audiences that attracted the likes of Sir Thomas Beecham, T.S. Eliot, violist Lionel Tertis, the Sitwells, T.E. Lawrence and Frederick Delius, who wrote his *Dance for the Harpsichord* for her.

Violet Gordon Woodhouse died in London and was buried in Folkington churchyard. *The Times* said, 'the subtlety of her playing was infinite and her clarity perfection… when she began to play, one became… entangled in a golden web of purest sound'.

Violet Gordon Woodhouse's Top Place
◐ *Folkington Manor: Gwynne family home*

Violet Gordon Woodhouse's Top Works
◐ *Pearl CD (GEMM CD9242) contains virtually all Violet Gordon Woodhouse's extant recordings, including:*
 Scarlatti: Keyboard Sonata in D major, Kk.29
 Scarlatti: Keyboard Sonata in A major, Kk.113
 Bach: Italian Concerto in F major, BWV.971 (1st and 2nd)
 Anon.: 'Woe betyd my wearie bodie'
 Bach: Well-Tempered Clavier (Book 1), Prelude and Fugue number 1

VIRGINIA WOOLF

1882-1941

RODMELL

Virginia Woolf was born in London, the third daughter of Leslie Stephen, literary critic and founding editor of the *Dictionary of National Biography*, and sister of Vanessa Bell (*see p.10*). She was taught at home, mainly by her father, and was a bookish and intellectual child, who wanted to write from an early age. She was close to her father, spending time in his study and going for long walks with him, which instilled her lifelong love of walking.

Both Virginia's parents had children from previous marriages, and one of her stepbrothers sexually abused her. She was already an emotionally fragile child – she suffered severe depression throughout her life – and not surprisingly this had a profound affect on her attitude towards men. Her mother died in 1895, closely followed by her half-sister and a much-loved aunt: by the time Virginia was 15, she was already writing about her own wish to die. Her father's death in 1904 tipped her into a serious mental breakdown and her first suicide attempt.

In 1904 Virginia, with Vanessa and their brothers Thoby and Adrian, moved into Gordon Square, Bloomsbury. Their home became the focus for the extraordinary group of writers, intellectuals and artists known as the 'Bloomsbury Group' and the setting for an avant-garde existence. Virginia had been writing since childhood and in 1906 completed a story called 'Phyllis and Rosamond', an account of two girls who, like herself and Vanessa, had escaped the constraints of their Victorian upbringing.

Lytton Strachey, one of the Bloomsbury Group, proposed to Virginia in 1909, even though he was gay, but she refused him. Three years later she married Leonard Woolf, a former colonial civil servant. As a Jew, a non-literary figure and heterosexual, he was somewhat outside the

Bloomsbury experience, but to gain Virginia he abandoned his career to write: she introduced him to her friends as her 'penniless Jew'. Working from London and Sussex, where Virginia rented Asheham House, they embarked on a joint writing career. The marriage was sexually confused and Virginia could be anti-Semitic, but they were close and Leonard supported Virginia through many illnesses.

In 1915 she published her first novel, *The Voyage Out*, which received a good response. The strain of marriage and publication, however, sparked two further breakdowns. Virginia and Leonard were now living in Hogarth House, Richmond, and in 1917 he bought a printing press, partly to divert Virginia, and they set up their own press – the Hogarth Press. From now on, all Virginia's books were published by the Hogarth Press. They also published T.S. Eliot, Katherine Mansfield, Maxim Gorky and were first to publish Sigmund Freud in English.

Virginia's second novel was *Night and Day*: its main character, Rosamond, was based on Vanessa and took as its theme the nature of women, something that constantly recurred in Virginia's work. The following years were a period of good health, during which Virginia wrote essays criticising Victorian novelists and explored a more modern writing style. In 1922 she published *Jacob's Room*, which marked a turning point in her style, made her a celebrity and identified her as a modernist. Over the next few years she published the novels that established her as one of the 20th century's most important writers: *Mrs Dalloway* (1925), *To the Lighthouse* (1927) and *The Waves* (1931).

Through her writings and through her personal life, Virginia Woolf displayed her admiration for and love of women. In 1928 she had an affair with Vita Sackville-West, immortalised in her novel *Orlando*, where the main character switches between male and female over time. In 1929 she published *A Room of One's Own*, which is seen as a feminist treatise and includes the now-famous phrase 'A woman must have money and a room of her own if she is going to write fiction.' Virginia actively supported the work of the Women's Co-operative Guild, encouraging them to publish letters on pregnancy and birth from working-class women and, encouraged by Ethel Smyth (whose advances she rejected), wrote a series of feminist essays, later published as *The Years*. As a pacifist, in *Three Guineas* she attacked war as a male plaything and made the point that even in 1938, when it was published, a whole range of professions were closed to women.

Virginia spent a lot of time in Sussex. In 1919 she had bought Monk's House, in Rodmell, and in 1940, when their London house was bombed, she and Leonard moved down there permanently. She always found it easy to write in Sussex and wrote an essay called 'Evening Over Sussex: Reflections in a Motor Car' that started: 'Evening is kind to Sussex, for Sussex is no longer young, and she is grateful for the veil of evening as an elderly woman is glad when a shade is drawn over a lamp, and only the outline remains.' The essay describes 'pink clouds over Battle', 'mottled, marbled' fields and used the landscape as a backcloth to explore her own thoughts about what she saw as her different selves and to speculate on how Sussex would be 500 years in the future.

Virginia Woolf was a well-known sight in the area, striding around the countryside, but was seen as very eccentric. Both she and Leonard feared a German invasion, and in 1940 Leonard, as a Jew, planned for their joint suicide should it happen. Unknown to them, they were in fact on Himmler's list for instant arrest. Virginia was still intending to live, but her depression set in again and she feared she was going mad. On March 28th 1941 she left a very affectionate note for Leonard, jammed a heavy stone into her pocket and drowned herself in the River Ouse. Her body was found three weeks later and her ashes were scattered in the garden of Monk's House.

Virginia Woolf's Top Places
- Monk's House, Rodmell: now owned by the National Trust
- Sissinghurst Castle, Kent: contains the original Hogarth printing press

Virginia Woolf's Top Works
- Mrs Dalloway, 1925
- To the Lighthouse, 1927
- Orlando, 1928
- A Room of One's Own, 1929
- The Death of the Moth, 1942: contains the essay on Sussex

FURTHER READING
& USEFUL WEBSITES

General

FISHERMEN OF HASTINGS: *200 years of the Hastings fishing community*, Steve Peak (NewsBooks, 1985)

HIGHWAYS AND BYWAYS IN SUSSEX, E.V. Lucas (Macmillan, 1904, 1912)

HISTORIC HASTINGS: *A Tapestry of Life*, J. Manwaring Baines (Cinque Port Press, revised edition 1986)

NOTABLE WOMEN OF VICTORIAN HASTINGS, Helena Wojtczak (The Hastings Press, 2002)

SUSSEX IN FICTION, Richard Knowles (Country Books, 2003)

SUSSEX WOMEN: *Famous, Infamous, Unsung*, Sharon Searle (JAK Books, 1995)

WOMEN OF VICTORIAN SUSSEX, Helena Wojtczak (The Hastings Press, 2003)

Specific

CHARLOTTE SMITH: *A Critical Biography*, Lorraine Fletcher (Macmillan, 1998)

A CHRONOLOGY OF THE LIFE AND WORKS OF SHEILA KAYE-SMITH, Michael Bristow-Smith (Sheila Kaye-Smith Society, 3rd edition 2005)

CLARA BUTT: *Her Life-Story*, Winifred Ponder (London, 1928)

LEE MILLER'S WAR, Anthony Penrose (Condé Nast Books, 1992)

THE LIVES OF LEE MILLER, Anthony Penrose (Thames & Hudson, 1985)

VIOLET: *The Life and Loves of Violet Gordon Woodhouse*, Jessica Douglas-Home (The Harvill Press, 1996)

VIRGINIA WOOLF, Lyndall Gordon (Virago, 2006)

VIRGINIA WOOLF, Hermione Lee (Vintage paperback, 1997)

A VISION OF EDEN: *The Life and Works of Marianne North* (Michael Joseph in collaboration with the Royal Botanic Gardens, Kew, 1980)

THE WORKS OF CHARLOTTE SMITH, ed. Stuart Curran (Pickering & Chatto, 2005)

WRITING AT THE KITCHEN TABLE: *The Authorized Biography of Elizabeth David*, Artemis Cooper (Penguin paperback, 2000)

Websites

uk.geocities.com/trevormidgley/ReleasedRecordings.html
Lists all of Clara Butt's recordings.

www.a2a.org.uk
An excellent website for historical research; links into the East and West Sussex archives. Anyone can visit the archives in Lewes, but it is advisable to make an appointment in advance.

www.leemiller.co.uk
Includes a virtual tour of some of Lee Miller's war photography.

www.womenofbrighton.co.uk/index.htm
Includes Brighton women mentioned in this book, plus many others.

INDEX

Acknowledgements

With thanks to Sharon Searle and Helena Woyjtczak for permission to call on some of their material; Mrs Verena Hanbury for talking to me about her grandmother, Dame Grace Kimmins; and the churchwarden at Rotherfield Church for information about Sophia-Jex Blake.